MANAGING
PROJECTS
FOR VALUE

The books in the Project Management Essential Library series provide project managers with new skills and innovative approaches to the fundamentals of effectively managing projects.

Additional titles in the series include:

Effective Work Breakdown Structures, Gregory T. Haugan

Project Planning and Scheduling, Gregory T. Haugan

Managing Project Quality, Timothy J. Kloppenborg and Joseph A. Petrick

Project Measurement, Steve Neuendorf

Project Estimating and Cost Management, Parviz F. Rad

Project Risk Management: A Proactive Approach, Paul S. Royer

www.managementconcepts.com

MANAGING PROJECTS FOR VALUE

John C. Goodpasture

MANAGEMENTCONCEPTS

Vienna, Virginia

fff
MANAGEMENTCONCEPTS
8230 Leesburg Pike, Suite 800
Vienna, VA 22182
(703) 790-9595
Fax: (703) 790-1371
www.managementconcepts.com

Printed in the United States of America

Library of Congress Cataloging-in-Publication Data

Goodpasture, John C., 1943–
    Managing projects for value / John C. Goodpasture.
        p. cm. — (Project management essential library)
    Includes bibliographical references and index.
    ISBN 1-56726-138-8 (pbk.)
    1. Project management. I. Title. II. Series.
HD69.P75 G665 2001
658.4′04—dc21

                                            2001044422

About the Author

John C. Goodpasture is a certified Project Management Professional with broad practical experience in executive management, project management, system engineering, and operations analysis in both industry and government. As founder and chief consultant at Square Peg Consulting, he specializes in customized application and delivery of project management, business process analysis and characterization, and training of project practitioners.

A graduate of Georgia Tech, John has proven hands-on executive, functional, and project management experience from assignments as vice president of a document archive and imaging operations group at a Fortune 500 company, director of a strategic project office, and director of a system engineering program office with responsibility for a multi-million dollar software systems product line at a major corporation. He began his career in the Department of Defense, where he had system engineering and program management responsibility for highly technical defense and intelligence systems.

He has developed unique techniques in his field, many of which are described in numerous papers he has authored on the subject of project management. Adept at personal communication and simplification of complex ideas, he has developed and delivered project training to numerous project and functional teams working in many different countries in the fields of information management, manufacturing, production operations, and software development.

This book is dedicated to my wife, Ann,
for her unlimited patience and encouragement,
without which this project
could never have been completed.

Table of Contents

Preface

Every individual endeavors to employ his capital so that its produce may be of greatest value. He generally neither intends to promote the public interest, nor knows how much he is promoting it. He intends only his own security, only his own gain.

—ADAM SMITH, *The Wealth of Nations, 1776*

This book discusses "managing projects for value" and the very important need for business and organizational involvement with projects. Truly successful project managers understand that projects exist only to promote and benefit the organization at large. The point of this book—and a motivation for writing it—is to communicate that the primary source of value for projects is the accomplishment of business objectives.

Understanding where value comes from is critical to satisfying those who charter and fund projects. Projects are not the everyday business of most businesses.* Projects are unique endeavors and, for many, a little bit mysterious. They are guided by methodologies and doctrine not familiar to those outside the domain of project management. Likewise, business practices, focused as they are on day-to-day operations, are not ordinarily employed or completely understood by project managers.

It follows then that the successful project manager must understand enough of the business goals and practices of an organization to translate business values into project values. This book provides the fundamentals that

---

*Used in this context, "business" refers to organizations of all types, including government, not-for-profit, volunteer, and the traditional profit-earning enterprises. For many businesses, such as construction, consulting, and product development, projects are the day-to-day business and lifeblood of operations. For all the rest, projects are employed to change the business but are not at the core of operations.

have proven successful in managing the intersection of project and business goals.

The usual case is that projects are undertaken only to satisfy a need that cannot be otherwise met. Needs are contained in a space called "opportunity." Opportunity is the vessel that holds all the needy and valuable things a business can do. Extracting value from opportunity for the benefit of stakeholders is the purpose of businesses and organizations. Extracting value from opportunity requires a determined application of effort and a commitment of resources.

To this end, organizations first apply their resources to day-to-day operations. Often, daily operations are incapable of exploiting opportunity with the options available—development, replacement, updating, or optimization. Projects are sometimes needed to maximize the extraction of value from opportunity. Projects are organized sets of nonrecurring tasks employed to do one thing one time. Projects consume resources—resources that might be otherwise employed to the benefit of the organization.

A project, once chartered and begun, represents a value judgment about needs and resources. When the project is successfully completed, the organization is that much better positioned to realize its vision. Managing for value then becomes the project management mission.

OUTLINE OF THIS BOOK

This book is organized into six chapters that take the project manager through a loosely coupled workflow. It begins with a general discussion of a project as an investment exposed to the normal dynamics of risk and reward; it concludes with a review of the mechanics of evaluating risk relative to project implementation and measuring the satisfaction of business goals. The following topics are covered in the chapters:

- *Chapter 1—Understanding Project Value.* Introduction of the five concepts of projects as investments; explanation of the three primary financial measures of project investments.
- *Chapter 2—The Sources of Value for Projects.* Introduction and development of the concept that valuable projects are the consequence of strategic planning and an instrument of strategy; explanation of a strategic planning workflow model useful for identifying projects.
- *Chapter 3—Balancing Investment, Returns, and Risks.* Application of a decision framework for selecting projects after strategic planning; introduction of a tool for project value evaluation—the project balance sheet.

- ***Chapter 4—Estimating the Future.*** Methods to determine scope, evaluate gaps, and analyze project capabilities to deliver value.
- ***Chapter 5—Delivering Value.*** Earned value methods to evaluate accomplishment and forecast successful completion of the project.
- ***Chapter 6—Schedule Risk and Value Attainment.*** Statistical methods to manage time (the most important factor in successfully delivering value), establish metrics, and measure performance of value attainment after project completion.

Projects are valuable because they are an important means to extract value from opportunity by managed application of resources.

John C. Goodpasture

Acknowledgments

would like to acknowledge the many people who assisted me with this book, including Ginger Levin, who got me started; Cathy Kreyche, who answered all my questions and guided me through the process at Management Concepts; and especially Dr. David T. Hulett, founder of Hulett Associates in Los Angeles, who has been of inestimable value over many years in assisting me in the art and science of risk management. I am indebted to Jonathan Goodwin of Shaw Industries, Inc., for his insightful discourse with me on the various topics in this book. And last, but by no means least, my mother, Dapheene, who came out of retirement as an editor to assist me in putting the right words in the right places.

CHAPTER 1

Understanding Project Value

Whether stated or implied, every organization has some purpose or mission that drives achievement. Likewise, each possesses some vision for the future that inspires, motivates, and attracts stakeholders. From vision and mission, opportunity can be revealed. To exploit opportunities, goals are developed.

CONCEPTS IN MANAGING PROJECTS FOR VALUE

Five key concepts guide the management of projects for value.

Concept 1: Projects Derive Their Value from Goal Achievement

Goals represent that portion of the opportunity value that can be transferred into the business. Goals are the state or condition to which organizations aspire; thus, value is attached to their achievement. Insofar as proposed projects are deemed necessary to achieve goals, projects are valuable to the organization (see Figure 1-1).

Said another way, projects are not valuable in and of themselves; they only acquire value from the role they play in exploiting opportunity. This idea forms the first of five concepts in managing projects for value: A project's value is derived from the value obtained by reaching goals (Figure 1-2).

Concept 2: Projects Are Investments Made by Management

By definition, projects begin and projects end,[1] but business goes on. For projects to exist, a deliberate assignment of resources must occur. In return for these resources, there is an expectation of a deliverable with benefits attached. Thus, projects can be seen as investments: principal applied, time expended, and return expected. For purposes of this book, the project sponsor is the project investor with authority to commit resources and charter the project. The charter becomes the investment agreement, specifying the value expected, the risk allowed, the resources committed, and the project manager's authority to apply organizational resources.

FIGURE 1-1   Business goals are the source of value for projects

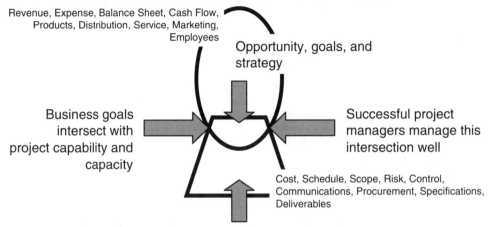

Revenue, Expense, Balance Sheet, Cash Flow,
Products, Distribution, Service, Marketing,
Employees

Opportunity, goals, and strategy

Business goals intersect with project capability and capacity

Successful project managers manage this intersection well

Cost, Schedule, Scope, Risk, Control,
Communications, Procurement, Specifications,
Deliverables

Project practices, methods, and values support and benefit the business

FIGURE 1-2   Concepts in managing projects for value

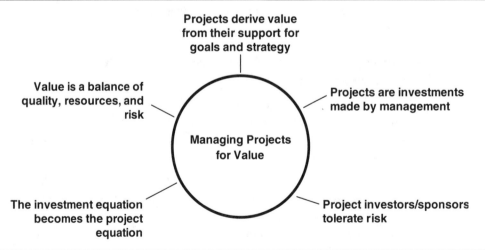

Projects derive value from their support for goals and strategy

Value is a balance of quality, resources, and risk

Projects are investments made by management

Managing Projects for Value

The investment equation becomes the project equation

Project investors/sponsors tolerate risk

Concept 3: Project Investors/Sponsors Tolerate Risk

The concept of investment is that a commitment is made in the present time with an expectation of a future reward. The displacement of the future from the present introduces the possibility that unfavorable outcomes could occur (see Figure 1-3). *Risk* is the word used to capture the concept of potentially unfavorable outcomes. Project sponsors, acting as investors, embrace and understand risk as an unavoidable aspect of pursuing reward. Although project investors/sponsors "tolerate" risk, they do not manage it. Instead, the project manager manages the risk of achieving successful deliverables. Once the project itself is complete, a "benefits manager" manages the risk of achieving the operational value of the project.

As individuals, project investors/sponsors have different attitudes regarding risk. For instance, "objective" investors/sponsors are indifferent to the specific nature of risk, judging only the risk-adjusted value. In effect, different risks of the same value or impact are judged equally.

Risk-averse project investors/sponsors seek a balance of risk and reward. Risk-averse investors/sponsors are not necessarily risk avoiders, but they do avoid risks that cannot be afforded if the risk comes true, or cost more if the risk comes true, than the value of the "try."

FIGURE 1-3   Time adds uncertainty to outcomes

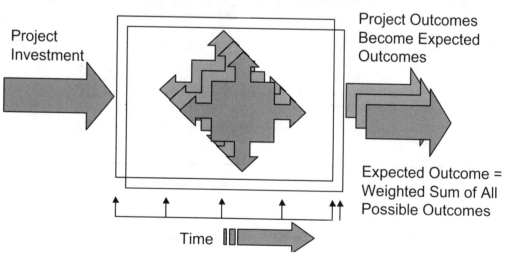

Project Performance, Time, Resources

Project Investment

Project Outcomes Become Expected Outcomes

Expected Outcome = Weighted Sum of All Possible Outcomes

Time

The following example illustrates this concept. In a coin toss, the bet is that heads gets $200 and tails gets $0. The expected value is $100 since half the time $200 will come up and half the time $0 will come up. The "value of the try" is negligible; nothing but a little time is lost if tails comes up. Suppose the bet is changed so that heads gets $400 and tails pays $200 for the same average outcome of $100. The risk-averse investor may not play the second bet even though it has the same positive expected value as the first because of the investor's aversion to even a 50 percent chance of losing $200 and a judgment that the entertainment "value of the try" is not worth $200.[2]

Figure 1-4 illustrates the concept of risk aversion applied to projects. Even though Project 2 has a higher expected return, its risk is beyond a threshold of affordable risk compared with Project 1. The risk-averse manager will approve Project 1 and disapprove Project 2.

Concept 4: The Investment Equation Becomes the Project Equation

The traditional investment equation of "total return equals principal plus gain" is transformed into the project equation of "project value is delivered from resources committed and risks taken." This equation is the project manager's "math." Many persons use the terms "benefits," "return," and "value" somewhat interchangeably even though they have different meanings.

FIGURE 1-4   To be risk-averse means there are risks that will not be taken

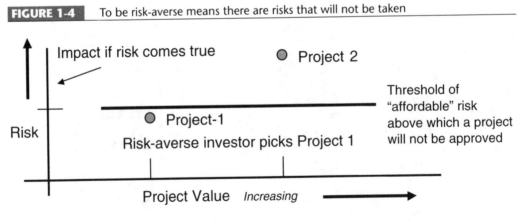

There are some risks a risk-averse project investor will not take. Project 2 will not be approved because its risk is "unaffordable."

This book employs the following definitions:

- **Benefits** are the mechanism for recovering project investment. For example, a project might be chartered to reduce production costs. Reduced production costs are the benefits that pay for the project investment.
- **Return** is the rate of change of a financial metric; for example, percentage incremental profit per period generated after the project is completed.
- **Value** is the need being satisfied by the project and the source of improved wealth in the business. In this project example, the business need may be to retain the production capability for customer satisfaction.

Concept 5: Value Is a Balance of Quality, Resources, and Risk

"Balance" is another term for equation. It is the state achieved when one side equals the other. In this context, quality demands are balanced or "provided" by resources and risk. Quality is used here in the sense of satisfying all dimensions of customer and stakeholder needs and expectations. Achievement of quality is accompanied by risk. How much risk? The answer is: only as much as is required to balance quality with resources (see Figure 1-5).

FIGURE 1-5   Value is a balance of quality, resources, and risk

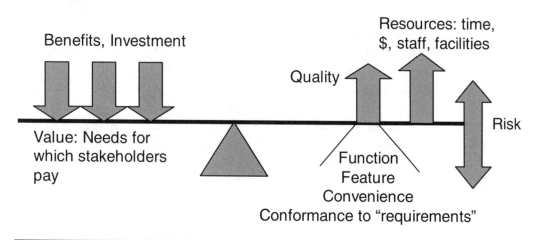

DIMENSIONS AND MEASURES OF VALUE

How is value dimensioned, and how is it measured? For most organizations, money is the objective measure of value. Consider this definition from James Anderson, Dipak Jain, and Pradeep Chintagunta: "Value . . . is the worth in monetary terms of the economic, technical, service, and social benefits a customer . . . receives in exchange for the price it pays for a market offering."[3] Money (or money equivalents) is consideration given for the value provided.

Quality Dimensions of Value

Quality, and therefore value, is multidimensional. Quality often is considered in terms of compliance with standards, applicability to function and use, effectiveness of cost, timely and convenient availability, and responsiveness to context and environment. Some quality measures also include satisfaction of unspoken need. Regardless of the dimension used, in the final analysis, quality represents the value worth paying for.

> *"In competitive terms, value is the amount buyers are willing to pay for what a firm provides them."*[4]

Consumers Value the Outcomes of Processes

Projects are often chartered to design and deliver improved processes and organizational functionality. Michael Hammer,[5] noted business process authority, consultant, and author, defines process this way: "Process: an organized group of tasks that together create customer value." By convention, processes are categorized as value adding (VA) or non–value adding (NVA).

A value-adding process begins with materials or information in a form not useful to users, applies a process to them, and produces a product or service that is useful. Consider this industrial VA process: Iron ore is mined and made into steel; the steel is then made into automobiles. Michael Porter uses the term *primary activities* to describe VA processes: "Primary activities . . . are the activities involved in the physical creation of the product and its sale and transfer to the buyer as well as after-sale assistance."[6] The beneficiaries of value-added processes are consumers—customers or users who can be internal or external to the organization. If these benefits are not dollar-denominated, as many may not be, then the "with-without principle" (discussed in detail in Chapter 3) is used to quantify process values in dollars.

MONETARY MEASURES OF VALUE

Value can be measured monetarily in several ways; these methods are developed in depth in many books and journals. Figure 1-6 illustrates three of these measures that are important to project managers. Their value lies in the fact that an otherwise straightforward calculation of cost and benefit often fails to represent project value correctly. Financial investment analysis techniques are required because:

- Projects take time to execute, and money is less valuable in the future. Therefore, the time value of money needs to be taken into account to estimate properly the value of outlays and benefits.
- Project investors have other choices for their investment dollars. It is often necessary to demonstrate to investors that a particular project is a good choice for investment.
- The future is subject to many outcomes, and each outcome potentially risks the value of the project.

Net present value, economic value add, and expected monetary value take these factors into account.

FIGURE 1-6   Time adds uncertainty to outcomes

Present value [PV] = Value at future date * Discount factor

Discount factor = $1/(1-k)^n$ **Where n is the number of accounting periods between the present and the future and k is the cost of capital factor**

➤ Net present value [NPV] = Σ PV of cash inflows -Σ PV of cash outflows

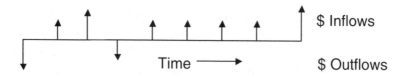

$ Inflows

Time ⟶ $ Outflows

➤ Economic value add = After tax operating income - k (Capital invested)
         Where k is the cost of capital rate, %

➤ Expected monetary value = Σ Outcome_{Nth} * Probability_{Nth}
         for all possible outcomes

Net Present Value

Net present value (NPV) is a calculation of cash value over a period of time. The NPV calculation is first applied to projects during the approval or selection process; later it is applied when there are scope changes that affect resources or the benefits stream. NPV captures two important concepts for the project manager:

1. The value of money decays over time. This decay is due to the effects of inflation, the uncertainty that future flows will continue or begin, and the uncertainty that a better investment is available elsewhere. In all cases, the "present value" is more than the "future value."
2. The value of the project is the net of the present value of all the cash outlays for investment and inflows from operations and salvage.

Cash flow is money—cash—coming from a "source" and going to a "use." Referring to the Figure 1-6 graphical notations for cash flows, outlays (investments) are uses of cash; cash outlays are shown along the timeline as down-pointing arrows placed at the point in time when the flow occurs. Inflows (benefits) are sources of cash; cash benefits are shown as up-pointing arrows placed appropriately on the timeline.

Consider the first NPV concept stating that money has a time value. Project managers have a great deal to say about time. There are two time segments to consider:

1. The project implementation schedule. For the most part, the project schedule is in the hands of the project manager to develop and then to manage.
2. The operational life of the deliverable, which begins once project implementation is complete. This lifecycle is defined and developed by the project management team in the course of the project.

To evaluate a project investment properly, and the subsequent cash flows associated with operations and salvage, all cash values must be adjusted to a common timeframe, typically taken to be the present, by "discounting" the value of future funds. Discounting is a risk management measure for uncertainties in the future. The degree of discount is not ordinarily within the purview of the project manager. Discounting is accomplished by applying a weighting factor to each future period, compounding the factor at each period to take into effect the accumulation of time. Table 1-1 presents the relevant equations and demonstrates their application.

The significance of the net of the present value to project mangers is this: Successful projects are those projects that add value to the business. Value

TABLE 1-1	Net Present Value

The net present value (NPV) of project outlays and inflows is equal to the sum of their future value, times a discount factor, compounded for time periods. The discount factor is a number less than 1 that weights the future value for the risk and uncertainties of future events

$$\text{Present value (PV)} = \text{Future value}/(1 + \text{Discount factor})^n$$

where n is the number of discounted periods between present and future. The present time is represented by n = 0. Where n = 0, PV = Future value/1

$$\text{NPV} = \text{PV (Outlays)} - \text{PV (Inflows)}$$

For example, a $500 investment made now that yields a $1,000 benefit two years from now, at a discount factor of 10 percent, has a net present value of $326.45.

$$\$326.45 = -\$500/(1 + 10\%)^0 + \$1000/(1 + 10\%)^2$$

$$\$326.45 = -\$500 + \$826.45$$

is only added if the net of all cash flows is positive; otherwise, there is more value going out of the business than there is coming in.

> *Valuable projects have a positive NPV over their lifecycle.*

The discount factor that brings the NPV to exactly zero, thereby not adding dollar value but not detracting either, is called the internal rate of return (IRR). IRR is the upper bound of the discount for which the project adds financial value to the organization. Rewriting the equations in Table 1-1 leads to the following:

$$\text{PV} = \text{Future value}/(1 + \text{IRR})^n$$

Applying IRR as the discount rate,

$$\text{NPV} = \text{PV (Outlays)} - \text{PV (Inflows)} = 0$$

The IRR for the example given in Table 1-1 thus is 41.4 percent. It is the upper amount of any discount rate for which the NPV is 0 or greater. Figure 1-7 illustrates these principles.

Consider the following project management example. Paul is a project manager responsible for a warehouse management project estimated to cost $500K and return cash benefits of $650K. These benefits are planned to come in the form of reduced costs of $130K per year for five years, beginning in the second year. To simplify matters, the following business rules apply:

- The $500K will be expensed in one year, thereby avoiding capital budgeting and the complications of depreciation.
- All benefits are after-tax cash.

FIGURE 1-7 Money has a changing value over time

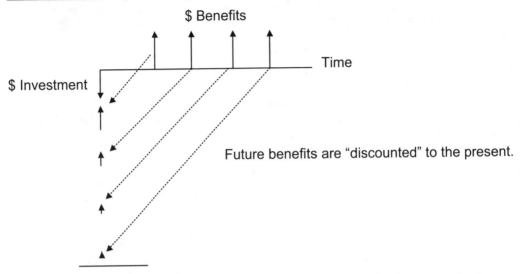

$ Benefits

Time

$ Investment

Future benefits are "discounted" to the present.

Σ NPV is the sum of benefits and investment in the present value.
IRR is the discount rate that makes this sum equal to $0.

Jim, Paul's finance manager, has an additional business rule: The project must have positive cash flow. In other words, it must have a positive NPV over a five-year lifecycle. The firm's discount rate is 12.8 percent for this type of project. From a table of present values, Paul finds that the benefits are worth less each year:

- At the *beginning* of the first benefit year, which is one year from the *beginning* of the project, the $130K benefit is only worth $115.25K ($130K discounted 12.8 percent for one year, calculated as $130K/(1 + 0.128)).

- As shown in Table 1-2, the sum of all the benefits in present value is only $459.48K. This amount is less than the $650K originally planned, and it is less than the $500K needed to have positive cash flow and meet Jim's criterion for acceptance. Unless benefits can be increased, the project will not be accepted.

On the other hand, if the discount factor could be as low as 9.43 percent, as shown in Table 1-3, then the NPV would be $0K and the project might be accepted. Thus, 9.43 percent is the IRR for the project.

Jim considers the 9.43 percent issue but states that it is unlikely that the discount factor can be reduced from 12.8 percent to 9.43 percent. Therefore, as shown in Table 1-4, to have the project accepted, annual benefits must be raised to approximately $141.46K per year. At this benefit value, the NPV, figured at a discount rate of 12.8 percent, will be $0K after five years. Paul will have to reevaluate the project scope to see if such a benefit stream can be realized.

TABLE 1-2 Paul's Project (1st Benefit Plan) ($000)

Year	Cash Investment	Face Value of Benefits	Benefits Present Value @ 12.8%	Present Value Cash Flow
0	($500.00)			($500.00)
1		$130.00	$115.25	($384.75)
2		$130.00	$102.17	($282.58)
3		$130.00	$90.58	($192.00)
4		$130.00	$80.30	($111.71)
5		$130.00	$71.19	($40.52)
Total	($500.00)	$650.00	$459.49	($40.52)

TABLE 1-3 Paul's Project (IRR of 1st Benefit Plan) ($000)

Year	Cash Investment	Benefits Face Value	Benefits Present Value @ 9.43%	Present Value Cash Flow
0	($500.00)			($500.00)
1		$130.00	$118.80	($381.20)
2		$130.00	$108.56	($272.64)
3		$130.00	$99.21	($173.44)
4		$130.00	$90.66	($82.78)
5		$130.00	$82.84	$0.06
Total	($500.00)	$650.00	$500.07	$0.06

TABLE 1-4 Paul's Project (2nd Benefit Plan) ($000)

Year	Cash Investment	Benefits Face Value	Benefits Present Value @ 12.8%	Present Value Cash Flow
0	($500.00)			($500.00)
1		$141.46	$125.41	($374.59)
2		$141.46	$111.18	($263.42)
3		$141.46	$98.56	($164.85)
4		$141.46	$87.38	($77.48)
5		$141.46	$77.46	($0.01)
Total	($500.00)	$707.30	$499.99	($0.01)

Economic Value Add

The second monetary value measure is economic value add (EVA).* EVA is closely related to NPV because both employ measures of discounted cash flow (DCF). EVA is a financial measure of how project performance, especially after the deliverables become operational, affects earnings.[9] Projects with positive EVAs earn back more than their cost-of-capital funding; that is, they return to the business sufficient earnings from reduced costs or increased revenues and margins to more than cover the cost of the capital required to fund these projects initially.

Cost of capital is an opportunity cost. It is not an expense on the project's expense statement. It is the "cost," used in the sense of return, that is "paid" to investors to keep them from taking their investments elsewhere to the next best opportunity. Capital is the "capital employed" or invested in the project that will be depreciated over time, as shown in Figure 1-8.

---

*P.T. Finegan[7] first wrote about EVA; it was made popular in a *Fortune* magazine article by Shawn Tully.[8] EVA™ is a trademark name registered by Stern Stewart & Company.

FIGURE 1-8   Economic value add (EVA) is a measure of profitability

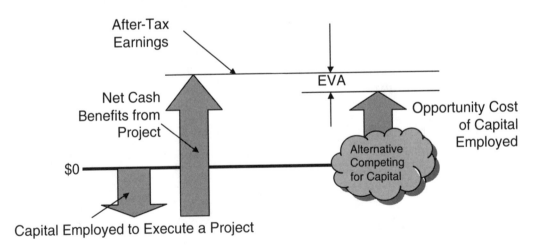

EVA = Present value of after-tax earnings—benefits from the next best competing opportunity

Capital and its cost are two important concepts from capital budgeting. The terms "discount factor" and "cost of capital" are used interchangeably in capital budgeting. Of course, capital budgeting is not employed in all organizations. In many government organizations, for instance, payments are expensed in the same year they are appropriated.

The logic of EVA is that if the business activity resulting from projects is not more profitable than the cost of capital the project consumes, then it may be more profitable, or at least equally profitable, and perhaps less risky, to invest the capital elsewhere.

EVA measures the economic performance of cash earnings. Earnings are what are reported as profit on the project's profit-and-loss (P&L) statement, but earnings are not all cash. P&L statements have many non-cash items on them; depreciation expense and expense accruals are two common entries. The examples that follow show how to take non-cash expenses into account.

"Profits are an opinion, but cash is a fact."[10]

Furthermore, a double entry for the capital outlay (on the cash flowsheet) and the capital depreciation (on the expense statement) must be avoided. Depreciation is simply the capital outlay distributed over time as an expense. Here are the rules for the project manager:

- Benefits, as used here, are measured as after-tax cash benefits.
- Depreciation, as a non-cash expense, through its impact on income tax cash payments, does have a cash benefit for taxable organizations by reducing the tax on gross benefits.
- Earnings and cash are related. Here are the equations:

$$\text{(Pre-tax operating cash benefits} - \text{Depreciation)} \times$$
$$(1 - \text{Tax rate)} = \text{After-tax earnings}$$

$$\text{Cash benefits} = \text{After-tax earnings} + \text{Depreciation}$$

In the second equation, cash benefits are also known as after-tax operating benefits. If the tax rate is 0 percent, as it would be for nonprofit and government organizations, then the equation becomes:

$$\text{Operating cash benefits} = \text{Cash benefits}$$

If the project is not a capital project, then also:

$$\text{Cash benefits} = \text{After-tax earnings}$$

Depreciation is not of consequence since it is not cash.

Consider the impact of EVA on Paul's warehouse improvement project if Jim imposes the requirement that the $500K investment be a capital investment depreciated over five years. Not only must the NPV be at least zero, but also the project must earn at least its cost of capital. Continuing with the warehouse project example, Table 1-5 is the depreciation schedule for Paul's project.

Now, to have an EVA equal to zero or better, after-tax earnings must at least be equal to CCE, the cost of capital employed. Proceed as follows:

- In equation form: EVA = After-tax earnings − CCE ≥ 0. In Paul's project, this equation requires that the present value of after-tax earnings be ≥ $146.55K, which is the PV of the cost of capital employed. (See Table 1-5 for PV CCE.)
- To simplify matters, assume that PV after-tax earnings will exactly equal $146.55K.
- Then, calculate the future value (FV) of the earnings to get annual figures to which depreciation can be added back. In the nth year, FV = PV × (1 + Discount factor)^n.
- Cash benefits equal this sum: FV (After-tax earnings) + Depreciation.
- NPV = PV (Outlays) − PV [FV (After-tax earnings) + Depreciation].

Table 1-6 summarizes the results. The first three rows calculate the EVA. Rows four through seven calculate the NPV. Notice that the PV of the EVA, as shown in the third row, is exactly 0. This result is a consequence of the assumption made that earnings will exactly equal the cost of the capital employed.

Table 1-6 illustrates an interesting result, which is shown below.

NPV (Cash flow) = Present value EVA (After-tax earnings)

This is not a coincidence of the figures used. It is a consequence of the relationships of cash flow and earnings after-tax.[11] Thus, it does not matter

TABLE 1-5 Depreciation Schedule for Paul's Project ($000)

Year 1	Year 2	Year 3	Year 4	Year 5	Total	
$100.00	$100.00	$100.00	$100.00	$100.00	$500.00	Depreciation
$500.00	$400.00	$300.00	$200.00	$100.00		Capital employed (CE)
12.80%	12.80%	12.80%	12.80%	12.80%		Cost of capital rate (CCR)
$64.00	$51.20	$38.40	$25.60	$12.80	$192.00	Cost of capital employed [CCE] = CE x CCR
$56.74	$40.24	$26.75	$15.81	$7.01	$146.55	PV CCE

TABLE 1-6 Paul's Project Plan with EVA = $0; Discount Factor 12.8% (3rd Benefit Plan) ($000)

Year 0	Year 1	Year 2	Year 3	Year 4	Year 5	Total	
($500.00)							Investment
	$56.74	$40.24	$26.75	$15.81	$7.01	$146.55	PC CCE
	$29.31	$29.31	$29.31	$29.31	$29.31	$146.55	PV after-tax earnings
	($27.43)	($10.93)	$2.56	$13.50	$22.50	$0.00	PV EVA
	$33.06	$37.29	$42.07	$47.45	$53.53	$213.40	FV after-tax earnings
	$100.00	$100.00	$100.00	$100.00	$100.00	$500.00	FV depreciation
	$133.06	$137.29	$142.07	$147.45	$153.53	$713.40	FV cash benefits
($500.00)	$117.96	$107.90	$98.99	$91.08	$84.07	$0.00	NPV cash benefits

to the project manager whether the criterion and measurement are NPV or EVA. Either will suffice for project selection and financial performance evaluation.

Before leaving the subject of EVA, several points are worth making. To be precise with EVA calculations, financial managers make adjustments for "equity equivalents" to restate the income statement in cash equivalents. This is a complex calculation beyond the scope of this book. A very readable treatment is given in Chapter 5 of the book *Value Based Management.*[12]

Expected Monetary Value

The third financial measure is expected monetary value (EMV). It is an NPV measure employed when more than one project outcome is possible, and each outcome has a different cost and schedule. Usually there can be only one figure for the project cost or schedule for which the project manager is responsible. In effect, a risk-averse estimate is needed for this "one figure." Risk-averse means that the risk is in balance with the reward, not that no risk exists. The "best point" estimate in the face of uncertainty is a statistic called "expected value."[13]

Expected Value

For the project manager, expected value is one of the most valuable statistics to know and apply. It is the best statistical estimate in the face of uncertainty. It is best in the sense that expected value is the only "unbiased" estimator of the average outcome of all possible outcomes. The group of "all possible outcomes" is called the "population." More often than not, the project manager cannot explicitly know all possible outcomes. However, an average outcome of all possible outcomes can be estimated. Unbiased estimator means that in the long haul, as more becomes known about the population, the estimate of the average will, in fact, turn out to be equal to the true average of the population.

> *If* μ *is the true average of the population,*
> *then as the sample size becomes "very large"*
>
> *Expected value* = μ

An unbiased estimator also is a "maximum likelihood" estimator. Maximum likelihood means that as more samples are taken of the population, the estimator continues to converge on a value. However, not all maximum likelihood estimators are unbiased.

Expected value is calculated this way: Each possible outcome of a task or work package is evaluated in monetary terms, with all monetary units discounted to their present value by the organization's cost of capital. Then, each present value outcome is weighted according to its probability of occurrence, where each probability or weight is a number between 0 and 1. The sum of all probabilities or weights must equal 1 exactly; if they do not, then not all possibilities have been considered, or too much weight has been given to one or more possibilities. These weighted outcomes are then summed into an expected value. By definition, expected value is the value of an outcome weighted by the probability of occurrence. Because each outcome is denominated in dollars, this expected value is called the expected monetary value. In the face of uncertainty, the project manager makes decisions to obtain the most favorable EMV.

Consider how Paul might employ EMV in his project. Paul must redesign his project to yield higher benefits than originally planned. Some risk must be taken to accomplish this goal. One approach might be to increase the face value of annual benefits to $170K, which is enough, but Paul estimates that there is only a 40 percent chance of success in achieving this figure. In fact, he estimates that there is a 60 percent chance that this approach will only yield $140K, which is not enough. Using expected value analysis, Paul finds that the EMV of this approach is $214K:

- 40% × $180K + 60% × $140K = $152K EMV
- The NPV of $152K in Paul's project is $37.24K, which is enough.

All other considerations being equal, Paul could justify taking a risk and adopting this approach on the basis of the EMV of its earnings.

- Projects are valuable because they are the means by which to extract value from opportunity by managed application of resources.
- Value, no matter how dimensioned and measured, is the intended outcome of investment.
- Risk objectivity means evaluating risk by the expected outcome, not necessarily the path to get there.
- Risk aversion means taking only those risks that are "affordable."
- Projects are investments. The project equation is: Project value is delivered from resources committed and risks taken.
- For most organizations, money is the objective measure of value. Three primary measures are employed for money values: net present value, economic value add, and expected monetary value.

NOTES

1. *A Guide to the Project Management Body of Knowledge, 2000 Edition* (Upper Darby, PA: Project Management Institute, 2000), Chapter 1, p. 4.
2. David T. Hulett. The example of risk aversion was provided to the author in a technical note from Dr. Hulett, 2000.
3. James C. Anderson and James A. Narus, *Business Market Management: Understanding, Creating, and Delivering Value* (Upper Saddle River, NJ: Prentice Hall, 1999), p. 5.
4. Michael E. Porter, *Competitive Advantage: Creating and Sustaining Superior Performance* (New York: Simon and Schuster, Inc., 1998), p. 38.
5. Michael Hammer. Seminar materials: *Managing the Process-Centered Enterprise: Principles and Practices* (Boston, MA: Hammer and Company, presented December 3-4, 1997), pp. 1-9.
6. Michael E. Porter, *Competitive Advantage: Creating and Sustaining Superior Performance* (New York: Simon and Schuster, Inc., 1998), p. 38.
7. P. T. Finegan, "Financial Incentives Resolve the Shareholder-Value Puzzle," *Corporate Cashflow*, October 1989, pp. 27-32.
8. Shawn Tully, "The Real Key to Creating Wealth," *Fortune*, September 20, 1993, pp. 38-50.
9. Robert C. Higgins, *Analysis for Financial Management* (Boston: Irwin/McGraw-Hill, 1998), p. 299.
10. Tom Pike, *Rethink, Retool, Results* (Needham Heights, MA: Simon and Schuster Custom Publishing, 1999), p. 177.
11. Robert C. Higgins, *Analysis for Financial Management* (Boston: Irwin/McGraw-Hill, 1998), p. 300.
12. John D. Martin and J. William Petty, *Value Based Management* (Boston: Harvard Business School Press, 2000).
13. John R. Schuyler, *Decision Analysis in Projects* (Sylva, NC: Project Management Institute, 1996), p. 11.

CHAPTER 2

The Sources of Value for Projects

Value increases when the satisfaction of the customer's need augments and the expenditure of resources diminishes.

—ROBERT TASSINARI
Le rapport qualite/prix, 1985

n its simplest form, *value* is a need to be satisfied for which someone is willing to pay or exchange other resources. Need can be tangible, as in a need for a product or service, or need can be qualitative, such as being timely and effective. Other needs can include conformance with performance requirements and cost, fitness to convenience and availability, and compliance with standards, among others. These are dimensions of quality.

The concept of quality has evolved greatly since the end of World War II when unparalleled consumer and business demand for technology and innovation entered America's economy.[1] The terms *quality* and *value* are often used interchangeably, although value is inescapably associated with price or cost-effectiveness. This book follows the convention that value is a balance between price (or resources) and quality. "Good value" is achieved for producer and consumer when there is a sense of equality and fairness between the value delivered and the resources expended.[2]

When: Value ≥ Price or Resources Expended
And Cost to Produce, Sell, and Service ≤ Price or Resources Expended
Then Value Delivered to Consumer "Balances" Value Earned by Producer

When need (i.e., something of value) cannot be satisfied by what is already available, or cannot be made available through the routine operations of the business or enterprise, then a project may be required. Project managers consider wants, needs, value, and quality as "requirements." As stewards of value and quality, project managers are customer-focused and outward-oriented. Unmet need is the source of requirements; it is the opportunity.

The challenge for project managers engaged in project planning is to separate those needs that truly generate value for the business from those that do not. It is critical to effective project investing to select projects and focus scope primarily on those value-generating needs. For instance, unmet customer needs whose satisfaction provides profitable revenues can be found. Operational inefficiencies that, if corrected, could improve financial performance and other measures of quality operations also can be identified.

Opportunity is the container for all things needed. Investing to satisfy identified need leads to reward. Mission provides the compelling call for action to exploit opportunity. Vision inspires and provides motivation. Vision coupled with mission exposes opportunity, unleashes innovation, and creates value. To effectively and wisely choose among opportunities, goal setting and strategic planning are required. Proposed projects are the likely outcomes of this process, as illustrated in Figure 2-1.

STRATEGY IS THE JOURNEY TO GOALS

Strategy is the term for the collective, actionable steps necessary to achieve goals and implement operating programs. Goals are destinations—

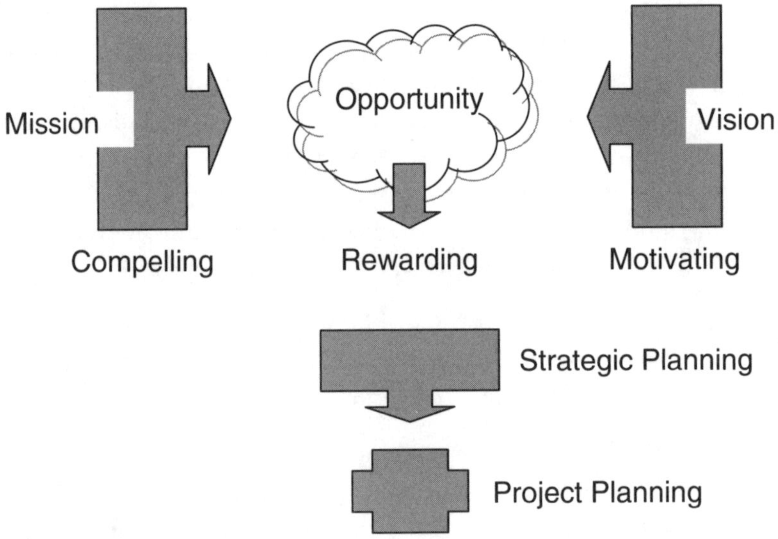

FIGURE 2-1   Mission opportunity and vision head project planning

not the journey to get there. Strategy is the journey. Goals are an expression of state—or the state of being—to which the organization aspires. As shown in Figure 2-2, goals, strategies, and operations are interdependent. Goals are achieved by the outcomes of strategy or the results of operations; then new goals are set, and the cycle repeats.

The Need for Change Drives Goal Setting

Goals are not static, at least not in organizations that are responsive to their environment; indeed, the bar for achievement is raised in almost every planning cycle. So it is that in organizations of all types, the constant watchwords are growth and change. In effect, growth is the goal; change is the strategy. But the questions are: How much growth? and Change in what direction?

Leadership and vision provide the direction. Pike, in his book *Rethink, Retool, Results*, writes: "The pinnacle role of the leader is to find the future."[3] Others have said that perhaps only a small fraction of a percentage of all the individuals in an organization are really responsible for what the group achieves. In an organization of hundreds, this is perhaps a handful of people. Set in the context of project management, the project manager and a small cadre of work unit managers are part of the leadership team responsible for creating the envisioned future.

FIGURE 2-2   Goal cycle repeats

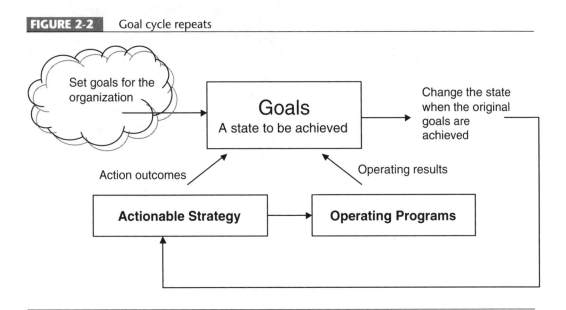

Vision is a name for the future. Vision is the uplifting, motivating call to the next level. Vision provides direction and purpose for mission. Vision exposes opportunity for the rewards it contains. Mission is transforming opportunity and transferring its rewards to the business. Harvesting reward from opportunity achieves goals. In effect, opportunity becomes a driver of goals.

The many disparate goals that are often developed in strategic planning must be organized and put into perspective. The "balanced scorecard," developed by Robert Kaplan and David Norton,[4] provides a helpful tool. In their model, goals are partitioned into four dimensions: financial, customer, internal operations, and learning and innovation (see Figure 2-3).

- Financial goals are the dollar-denominated goals that address finance and accounting outcomes of the business.
- Customer goals address how the customer views the business; the primary measure is customer satisfaction.

FIGURE 2-3   A balance of goals in four dimensions

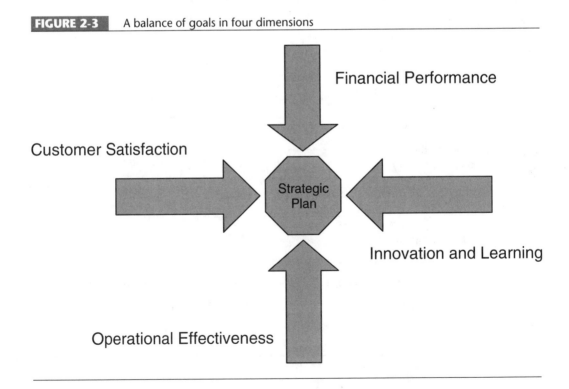

- Internal operational goals address process and functional performance excellence and the effectiveness of core competence. Measurements are largely internal, comparing performance with standards.
- Learning and innovation goals address product introduction and innovation, organizational learning and skill development, and application of technology and productivity tools.

Change As a Consequence of Opportunity

Growth is fueled by change and opportunity. Significant change is powered by innovation, which requires financial investment and incentive. Innovation often introduces new information, new process, and new technology; it often changes the organization's face to the customer, offering new services, products, and a different way of doing business. It also can optimize the way an organization delivers existing products and services. These innovations, in turn, may require new skills, new roles, or even new jobs.

Change is not just a one-time roll-out of something new, however. Change is an event followed by a process. The change process provides evaluation and continuous improvement until a new threshold of change is needed. Figure 2-4 illustrates the change cycle.

FIGURE 2-4   Change is an event followed by a process

Next Change

Change in process, tools, policy, and procedure occurs at an event

Innovation fuels change

Change in organizational behavior is a process of application, evaluation, and improvement over time

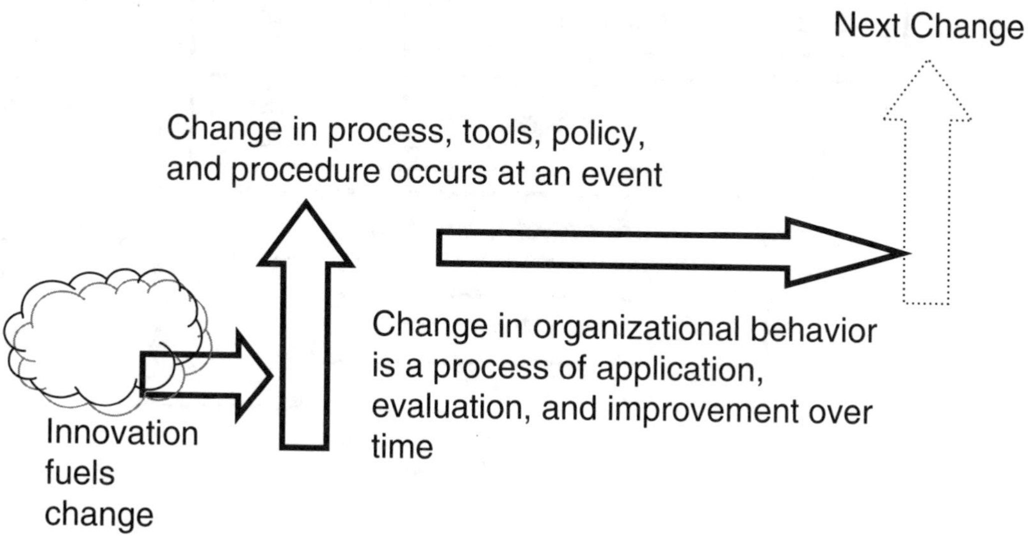

Change is a component of strategy, a necessary outcome of strategic planning. To act on strategy means to take action, and many actions combined take the form of projects. Projects are the instrument of strategy to effect needed change to accomplish goals.

SIX STEPS IN STRATEGIC PLANNING: FROM OPPORTUNITY TO PROJECTS

Projects are an important consequence of strategic planning. Opportunity, which is the source of value, is at the head of the planning process. Projects complete the planning cycle. Projects are derived from opportunity by means of goals and strategy.

A Model for Goal Deployment and Strategic Planning

Figure 2-5 shows a model for deriving goals from opportunity and creating a strategic plan. This model portrays decomposition of goals into

FIGURE 2-5 Projects derive value from their support for strategy and goals

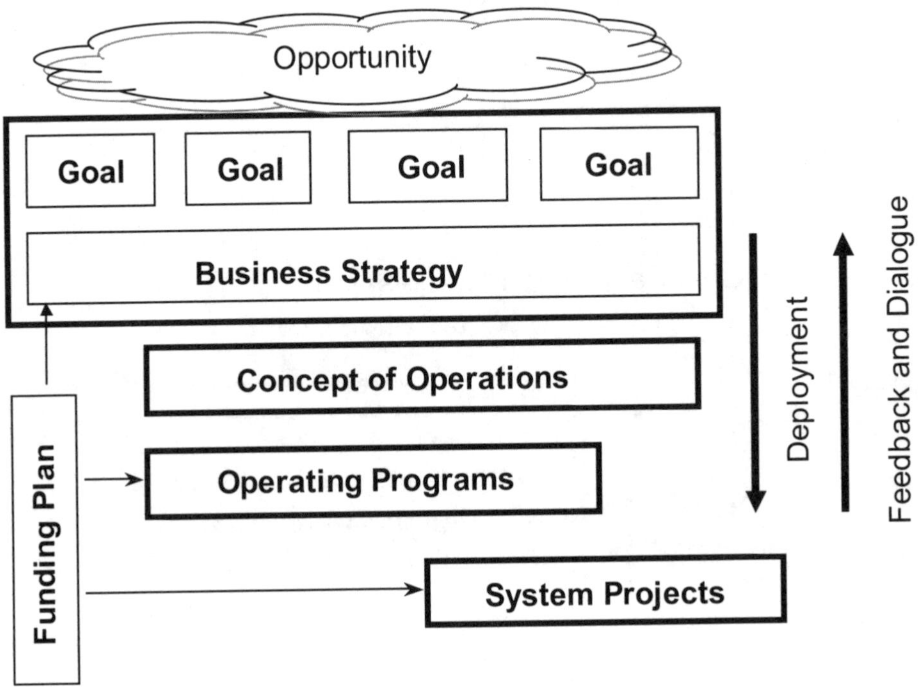

Adapted and reprinted from author's articles with permission from PMI®

strategy, operating concepts, programs, and projects.[5] The name given to this process is "goal deployment." Planning in this way is applicable to all levels of the organization.

Goals and business strategy at one level are decomposed into related entities at another level, and so on down the organizational ladder. These intermediate or departmental goals and strategies are *derived*; they flow down from the strategic plan. At the same time, bottom-up dialogue is added for real-time feedback, creating in effect a planning engagement. Figure 2-6 depicts this decomposition as applied to goals.

Step 1: Opportunity Identification

The purpose of opportunity identification is to discover value that adds wealth to the organization. Wealth can be in the form of added revenues, avoided costs, and lower taxes, all of which are directly measured in dollars. Yet, higher productivity, less turnover, less risk exposure, higher customer satisfaction, and other outcomes on the balanced scorecard also create wealth, even if not easily quantified in dollars.

FIGURE 2-6   Goals are allocated to departments

		Enterprise Goals		
		Financial Performance	**Product and Technology Innovation**	**Operational Effectiveness**	**Organizational and Staff Development**
Enterprise goal specifications →		X% return on new product investment	New product introduced	Operational effectiveness of 60% achieved	New product knowledge deployed
		Departmental goals are "integrated" by the enterprise			
	Department 1	New product research and development complete	Specified allocation of enterprise goals to departments		
	Department 2				
	Department 3		Marketing complete		All staff trained in new product knowledge

The project manager performs the following steps to identify opportunity:

- **List what is perceived to be valuable to the customer community.**
Describe what is known about needs and the "qualities" of the opportunity in terms of the many dimensions of value. Create a table to hold descriptions of function and use, performance, and price. Consider esthetics; esteem appeal; timeliness and convenience; and conformance to standards, ethics, regulation, and law. Include compatibility with products, environment, or other context as part of opportunity. Define need and value in terms of *what* really is valuable, to *whom* it is valuable, and *how valuable* it is.

- **Employ divergent thinking**; it spins out ideas rather than converges on solutions. Look at the opportunity from several points of view: customer, supplier, maintainer, user, trainer, or other stakeholder. Evaluate the dimensions already discussed for each of these views, grading each for importance. Use this test: If the feature, function, or attribute were provided, how compelling would its presence be and how much value would it add to the opportunity? If a feature, function, or attribute were missing or taken away, how distressful or less valuable would the opportunity be?

- **Apply brainstorming to expose as many ideas as possible**; this technique typically creates more ideas than can be used. Remove overlaps, duplicates, or conflicts. Group similar thoughts in the remaining ideas together. (These groupings are called "affinity groups.")

- **Summarize each affinity group** with a "headline" or abstract of the ideas contained in the group.

- **Validate, or confirm, opportunities with customers.** Remember that customers may be internal (e.g., end-users, trainers, maintainers) or external.

- **Develop a plan for what is to be accomplished before approaching customers.** The book *Customer Visits*[6] proposes that the elements of this plan include written objectives for the interview; a preview of what classes of customers, even if internal, are going to be addressed; an interview outline or discussion guide that contains the points to be validated; and a follow-up plan for using the information.

- **Collect the "voice of the customer"** as literally as possible. Observe and record the context, the environment, and the unspoken communications.

- **"Process" the customer interviews**, creating affinity groups of like statements with headline summaries. Include unspoken and contextual information in the relevant affinity groups as additional information.

- **Repeat the process** described above as often as necessary.

Table 2-1 summarizes the qualities of good opportunity identification.

Step 2: Goal Development

Goals are developed from opportunity. Recall the "Jesse James question" and paraphrase it as: "Why rob banks? Because, that is where the money is." Achievement of goals transfers value from the opportunity to the business or enterprise.

To develop goals, the following process should be followed:

- Adopt a date at which time the future condition or state must be achieved.
- Estimate from the opportunities identified the part of the opportunity that can be addressed by the organization's products and services.
- Determine what form the value of the opportunity will take when transferred to the organization. This value form will be the foundation for goal statements.
- Write statements that are quantified and provable (i.e., verifiable descriptions of the state or condition that will exist on the adopted date). An example statement would be: "Revenues in three years are to be $5 million annually."

TABLE 2-1   Qualities of Opportunity Identification

Attribute of Quality	Definition and Explanation
Fitness to function and need	Functionality is a description of behavior expected or needed, typically thought of as "capability" or "capacity." Function focuses on need, not on solution. Function can be "decomposed" from need, and then "recomposed" through validation into product or service.[7]
Compliance to standards, regulations, ethics, and law	Compliance is inward-focused on meeting the "letter of the law." In many instances, customers do not have a choice regarding the value of compliance.
Responsive to time, convenience, and space	This quality is essentially capacity. It can be the capacity to fulfill customer need, or the capacity to deliver a product or service that will fulfill customer need in a timely and convenient manner.
Appeal to presentation, appearance, and esteem	Attention to qualitative measures is often essential to the exploitation of an opportunity. Satisfaction is in the eye of the beholder; therefore, it is subject to the risk of "I'll know it when I see it."
Compatibility with context, as in environment, politics, legacy, and culture	In most respects, compatibility with context is a compliance concept but is often outward-focused on external constraints and conditions.

- Create a map (i.e., show a relationship) between the goal and the opportunity to chart value flow from the opportunity to the organization.

Step 3: Strategy Development

Strategy responds to goals. To develop strategy, conceive of the steps necessary to achieve the goal. It often is helpful to work backward from the goal, asking a series of "how" questions. Consider the following example: Goal (a statement of condition): "In 2001, revenues from new customers are to be $10 million annually." Strategy (actionable steps): How? "Acquire new customers with new products." How? "Develop one new product in each product line." How? "Discover and address unmet functionality."

Strategy is always expressed in an imperative sentence. For example, a strategy could be: "Develop five new products, one in each of five product lines." Effective strategy does not have to be too detailed. The project plan will provide the detail for each strategy step.

Strategy may, and usually does, have a many-to-many relationship with goals. Many-to-many means that one goal may be answered by more than one strategy step, and a strategy step may respond to more than one goal. Confusing? It could be. For this reason, a goal-to-strategy mapping table is a useful tool. Strive to maintain a "flat" mapping table. In a flat table, each cell or field can have only one entry. Multiple rows in the table may be required to keep the table flat. Flat tables can be easily sorted, filtered, and joined to create reports and "data views" for strategy managers. Table 2-2 is a flat goal-strategy map.

TABLE 2-2 Strategy Maps to Goals

Strategy		Goal Mapping			
Strategy ID	Strategy	1.0 Financial	2.0 Operations Effectiveness	3.0 Product & Technical Innovation	4.0 Learning & Staff Development
S-1	Introduce five new products	1.1 Revenue from new products	Not applicable	3.1 Product line refreshment	Not applicable
S-1	Introduce five new products	1.2 Revenue from new customers	Not applicable	3.1 Product line refreshment	Not applicable
S-2	Segment customers	1.2 Revenue from new customers	Not applicable	Not applicable	Not applicable

Note: This is an example of a "flat table." In a flat table, each cell has only one entry. Where the strategy maps to more than one goal, as in the first two rows, then a repeated row of strategy is provided.

Step 4: Concept of Operations

Develop and write a concept of operations in narrative form. The concept of operations explains how operations will do business when the actionable steps of strategy are completed. The concept of operations (ConOps) serves as a concept integration and validation tool. Like all validation tools, it helps to answer the question: "Is this [strategy or strategic plan] complete, accurate, and effective for the intended purpose?"

Typically, the ConOps identifies job, role, and task for each actor in the workflow. The information used or created by each task and actor is specified. Systems required to support the workflow are described. Measurements, validation techniques, and verification methods are likewise addressed. Error conditions, exceptions, and error recovery methods are usually included. Flowcharts, entity relationships charts, and state charts often supplement narrative in the ConOps.

Scenarios fill out the ConOps. A scenario is a specific workflow thread under specific conditions, inputs, and triggers. Scenarios are often entitled "A day in the life of. . . ."

Step 5: Operating Programs

Operating programs are the day-to-day sustaining activities that are the outcomes of strategy, or the outcomes of the projects chartered by strategy. Operating programs could include manufacturing, distribution, sales, and service associated with products and services. When the actionable steps of strategy are complete, the "memorial" to that work is a set of functional operating programs. The integrated effect of operating programs is explained in the ConOps. Table 2-3 illustrates the process of tracing programs to strategy.

TABLE 2-3 Operating Programs Map to Strategy

Operating Programs			Strategy Mapping	
Operating Program ID	Program Name	Concept of Operations	Strategy ID S-1	Strategy ID S-2
OP-1	Pg-1: New product launch and post launch evaluation	ConOp-1: How new products are launched after development	Introduce five new products	Not applicable
OP-2	Pg-2: Customer profiling and annual customer needs evaluation	ConOp-2: How customer needs and wants are maintained	Not applicable	Segment customers

The importance of operations to project management is that the benefits associated with projects are obtained by operations. The project itself is an investment, but at some point the benefits from operations pay back the investment.

Step 6: Project Identification

When a one-time endeavor is needed to implement a step of strategy, those tasks are collectively made into a project. The project manager's task in strategic planning often is to develop the project profile that will become the project charter. Projects developed in this way are instruments of strategy. As strategy is the means to goals, so, by extension, projects are a means to goals.

> *Project value is derived from the value of the goal; projects are valuable because of their support for strategy.*

One useful tool for the project manager is a tracking table to provide the traceability from goals to projects. Table 2-4 provides an example of such a table that shows the mapping from projects back to strategy.

In coordination with Tables 2-3 and 2-4, complete tracking of goal deployment is provided to projects and programs. Combining relevant rows from these two tables for projects PR-1 and PR-6 yields Table 2-5. This table shows the full deployment of PR-1 and PR-6 to the goals and strategy they support.

TABLE 2-4 Projects Map to Strategy

Projects		Strategy Mapping	
Project ID	**Project Deliverable**	**Strategy ID S-1**	**Strategy ID S-2**
PR-1	New product #1	Introduce five new products	Not applicable
PR-2	New product #2	Introduce five new products	Not applicable
PR-3	New product #3	Introduce five new products	Not applicable
PR-4	New product #4	Introduce five new products	Not applicable
PR-5	New product #5	Introduce five new products	Not applicable
PR-6	Customer database	Not applicable	Segment customers

TABLE 2-5 Projects Map to Strategy and Goal

Projects from Table 2-4		Strategy and Goal Mapping	
Project ID	**Project Deliverable**	**Strategy from Table 2-2**	**Goals from Table 2-2**
PR-1	New product #1	S-1 Introduce five new products	1.1 Revenue from new products
PR-1	New product #1	S-1 Introduce five new products	1.2 Revenue from new customers
PR-1	New product #1	S-1 Introduce five new products	3.1 Product line refreshment
PR-6	Customer database	S-2 Segment customers	1.2 Revenue from new customers

- Projects are an instrument of strategy. The value of projects is directly traceable to and flows from opportunity by means of strategic planning.
- Value is a need to be satisfied for which someone is willing to pay money or exchange other resources. Value is a balance between quality and resources, but acceptance of risk is often needed to achieve this balance.
- Value, no matter how dimensioned and measured, is the intended outcome of investment. The concept of investment is simple: commit resources to gain a return.
- Projects are an investment. Project managers act on behalf of project investors. The project manager's mission is to manage assigned resources to deliver the value expected, taking measured risks to do so.

NOTES

1. S. Shiba, A. Graham, and D. Walden, *A New American TQM: Four Practical Revolutions in Management* (Portland, OR: Productivity Press, 1993), Chapter 2.
2. Michel Thiry, *Value Management Practice* (Sylva, NC: Project Management Institute, 1997), p. 8.
3. Tom Pike, *Rethink, Retool, Results* (Needham Heights, MA: Simon and Schuster Custom Publishing, 1999), p. 13.
4. Robert S. Kaplan and David P. Norton, "The Balanced Scorecard: Measures That Drive Performance," *Harvard Business Review*, January-February 1992, pp. 73-79.
5. John C. Goodpasture and Thomas N. Mangan, "A Practical Methodology for Integrating Functional Process Design and Data-Driven Packaged Software Development," *PMI '98 Seminars and Symposium Proceedings* (Upper Darby, PA: Project Management Institute, 1998).
6. Edward F. McQuarrie, *Customer Visits* (London: Sage Publications, 1993).
7. Michel Thiry, *Value Management Practice* (Sylva, NC: Project Management Institute, 1997).

CHAPTER 3

Balancing Investment, Returns, and Risk

Facts do not cease to exist because they are ignored.

—ALDOUS HUXLEY

This chapter first addresses the task of selecting projects, building on the concepts introduced in Chapter 1. Then it introduces a tool called the project balance sheet, which is helpful in organizing investment, capability, and risk.[1] The goal deployment paradigm discussed in Chapter 2 provides a methodology for developing a portfolio of valuable projects. However, project investors/sponsors, working with project managers, often find that it is necessary to select only certain projects for execution, deferring or canceling others. Selecting projects requires a decision framework in which to work.

A decision framework consists of the following:
- A process for decision making
- Tools for gathering and analyzing data required by the process
- A decision policy for applying the data to the selection decision.

Once a project is selected, the project balance sheet holds the information the project manager uses to charter the project and negotiate scope, time, and resources with the project investors/sponsors.

SELECTING PROJECTS FOR INVESTMENT

By their very nature, all projects differ from one other. Some are more intuitively valuable than others. Intuition is important for recognizing project value where it may be otherwise obscured and for making quick choices in the face of overwhelming possibilities. However, at a more detailed level, and in the context of scarcity where choices must be made, intuition may not be enough for decision making. Therefore, a rational decision framework is needed.

> *Rationality means outcomes are more predictable from, and a consequence of, the application of input to process according to disciplined practices.*

Within such a framework, the value of any one project can be compared with an absolute standard, such as earning more than the cost of capital. The decision policy might be "pick only projects with positive economic value add." A project could be compared with other projects, and the decision policy could be to pick the project with the most favorable expected monetary value (EMV).

In this book, the decision policy will be to select projects that maximize returns to the business or optimize performance toward achieving the goals on the balanced scorecard.

Financial Scorecard

Some goals are intuitively more important to the success of the organization than others. What are these measures of organizational success with which project managers should be concerned? First, there is financial success, which for many organizations means increasing the well-being of all stakeholders. A common metric is profits, more exactly, "accounting profits," the profits calculated by accountants. (Accounting profit, which constitutes "after-tax earnings," was discussed in Chapter 1.)

> *Accounting profit = (Revenues − Expenses) × (1 − Tax rate),*
> *where expenses includes cost of goods sold, operating expenses,*
> *and interest expenses.*

It is evident from the equation that accounting profits do not consider risk, do not consider the time value of money, and do not account for the opportunity cost of capital. The idea of "economic profit" is thus introduced.[2]

> *Economic profit = Accounting profit − Cost of capital employed*

Notice that economic profit is for all practical purposes equivalent to economic value add (EVA). The upshot of this equation is that a company is not profitable unless it earns more than it takes from the available capital.

Most often project managers must evaluate their projects not only for EVA or economic profit performance, but also for accounting profit (return) performance. The three common metrics for accounting returns are:

1. **Return on sales (ROS).** ROS is perhaps one of the most common measures because it represents how well the business is obtaining a premium over cost for the value it is providing. ROS = Profit/Sales or ROS = Profit/Revenues.

2. **Return on assets (ROA).** ROA is a measurement of management effectiveness to create customer value by employing assets that are owned by the organization and provided to managers for their use. Figure 3-1 illustrates the value cycle of creating returns from assets entrusted to project managers. ROA = Profit/Assets.

3. **Return on investment (ROI).** ROI measures how well the project manager is performing on behalf of others to use their investment to create value in the business. ROI = Profit/Investment.

The effective employment of assets and investment is extremely important to a successful enterprise. Assets and investment are the fuels employed in projects by project managers. Consider the equations in Table 3-1, which illustrate the connectedness of these measures.

Application of the equations in Table 3-1 can have important impacts on project managers:

- Project managers really do have two bosses: the "owners," represented by project investors/sponsors, and the "customers," those who find value in the deliverables of the projects.

FIGURE 3-1   Projects are measured by return on assets

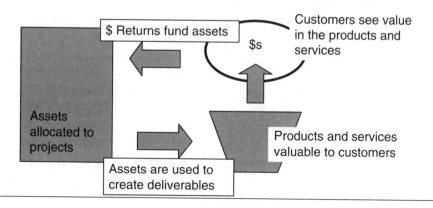

TABLE 3-1	Value Proposition for Customers and Owners Is Proportional

Profit margin is the premium for value that customers pay in excess of cost.	Equating Customer and Owner Values
	Standard measures:
	1. ROA = ROS × Sales/Assets
	  (Sales/Assets also is known as "asset turns.")
	2. ROI = ROA × Assets/Investment
	  (Assets/Investment also is known as "financial leverage.")
	Substitute these words:
	Value premium from customers for *ROS* and
	Value creation demanded by project investors/sponsors for *ROI*
	Rewriting equation 1 as equation 3, and equation 2 as equation 4:
	3. ROA = Value premium from customers × C_1
	4. ROA = Value creation demanded by project investors/sponsors × C_2
	where C_1 and C_2 are proportionality factors
	Combining equations 3 and 4:

The value propositions viewed by customers and investors/sponsors are proportional to each other.	5. Value creation demanded by project investors/sponsors = Value premium from customers × C_1/C_2 **Conclusion:** C_1/C_2 is dimensionally "Sales/Investment," which is "investment turns" or investment leverage. Interpret the above as: Value creation demanded by project investors/sponsors = Investment leverage on the value premium from customers

- Owner and customer interests are related by profit measures. The factor of proportionality is defined as C_1/C_2, which is the leverage of investment on sales.

Goals Scorecard

Beyond financial measures, other factors are meaningful to project success when both project implementation and follow-on operations are taken together. Of course, the project manager does not often have responsibility for operational success. The project manager's responsibility is to ensure that project implementation is consistent with operational goals and measures, in effect, doing the right thing right.

Table 3-2 shows an example of a strategic goals scorecard from a manufacturing company.

Take note that the goals for the XYZ Company are, for the most part, quantitative but do not have a value score per se. Ordinarily, increasing the wealth of stakeholders is the ultimate goal of profit-making enterprises. For these businesses, financial goals rank highest. For others, the scorecard could come out differently.

Measurable Criteria for Value Decisions

For purposes of making decisions about which projects to implement and which to defer or cancel, the project investors/sponsors need a set of

TABLE 3-2 Scorecard of Strategic Goals for the XYZ Manufacturing Company

Financial goal
- Earn 6 percent on sales, 18 percent on investment, and 13.6 percent on assets this year.

Customer satisfaction goal
- Provide a satisfaction greater than 95 percent on all indicators by year 3.
- Have customer returns of less than 1 percent of sales this year.

Operational effectiveness goal
- Achieve inventory turns of 8.7 or better in each of the next three years.
- Achieve major machine availability of 98.7 percent or better measured annually.

Learning and innovation goals
- Introduce one new product in each customer segment each year.

decision criteria. Project managers often participate in these decisions. These criteria must be consistent with a decision policy and measurable within a decision framework. Moreover, these criteria must be rational. "Rational" means that the decision is a predictable outcome of decision data applied to the deciding process. Consider the criteria shown in Table 3-3.

The first four criteria infer that the outcomes of all projects can be measured in dollar terms. Is this possible and practical to do? In general, the answer is yes, as explained by a principle from capital budgeting that is called the "with-without" paradigm.

The statement of the principle is: "Imagine two worlds, one in which the investment is made and one in which it is rejected. All cash flows that are different in these two worlds are relevant to the decision, and all those that are the same are irrelevant."[3]

For project managers, this principle provides a practical tool for estimating "soft costs" and "soft benefits." "Soft" refers to the fact that the con-

TABLE 3-3 Criteria for Selection of Projects

Attribute	Description
Net present value (NPV)	NPV ≥ 0. In present value terms, the project must add to the wealth of the business or organization by saving more in operating costs or creating new sources of cash or customer value in excess of the outlays needed.
EVA	EVA ≥ Cost of capital. The project must earn back its cost of capital.
EMV	The EMV of alternatives must be less favorable.
Returns	Project ROA, ROI, and ROS must not dilute the company's performance. Project is risk-affordable to project investors/sponsors: The expected value (cost, time, and performance) is in balance with project investors/sponsors' tolerance for the risk outcomes.
Risk	Project risk is judged objectively. Risk factors are evaluated by their expected value and made part of the EMV calculation.

nection between cause and effect cannot be unambiguously established. Examples of projects with soft costs or benefits are projects that improve personal productivity, increase revenue from existing customers with existing products, or improve functional effectiveness such as reduced hold-time in customer service call centers.

Consider this example of the with-without principle. The human resources department is to receive a new payroll system at a cost of $50K in capital. However, no specific hard benefits, like headcount reduction, are anticipated. Nevertheless, the system is justified as a "personal productivity" enhancer by virtue of its intuitive computer user interface. Tom H., the human resources executive, assembles his team to consider the impact of this new system in the "future state" of his department. Table 3-4 presents the results.

Personal productivity savings are soft since they are "unbudgeted" in the current budget. New hiring is soft since it is "avoided" in the next budget. Less overtime paid is a hard savings since the overtime currently budgeted can be reduced in the next budget cycle.

The last criterion listed in Table 3-3 is about fitting the project to the organization's tolerance for risk. Table 3-5 illustrates a project with risky

TABLE 3-4 With-Without Principle

As-Is Situation *without* New Payroll Project	Should-Be Savings *with* New Payroll Project
• No change in personal productivity; hire staff as needed	• Increased personal productivity in each task and job avoids hiring new staff ($45K for each staff member "avoided")
• Hire one manager	• Forego hiring one manager next year since managers will be able to have greater span if there are few productivity problems ($70K "avoided")
• Pay normal amount of overhead	• Less overtime paid ($20K less overtime put into budget)

TABLE 3-5 Risk Tolerance

Project Investor/Sponsor's Expectation	Face Value of Impact of Risky Outcome	Probability of Occurrence* (0%–100%)	Expected Impact (Face Value × Probability)
Deliverables will be on time and within budget	60-day delay	5%	3 days
	20-day delay	15%	3 days
	On-time delivery	80%	0 days
	Expected impact of identified risk		6 days

*The project manager estimates that a risky outcome will occur at this frequency or less (e.g., five times in 100 [5%] or less).

outcomes. How tolerant might the project investor/sponsor be in this situation?

Employing objective measures of risk, the project manager transfers six days' risk, an objective measure, to the project balance sheet. (The project balance sheet is a tool that will be discussed in subsequent chapters.) In doing so, the project manager takes note that the 60-day delay and the 20-day delay both have an expected value of 3 days, but if the risk comes true their impacts would be different. In fact, should the 60-day delay occur, and should a delay of 60 days be overwhelmingly damaging to project success, then a risk-averse project manger could not accept this possibility. Consequently, the project manager would have to redesign the project to avoid this possibility entirely or recommend rejecting this project as unacceptably risky according to the decision criteria contained within the decision policy.

Decision Policy for Selecting Projects

The best policy is one that can be followed in the majority of situations, presenting few exceptions to manage. "Manage to policy" is the mantra of the rational organization. For the project manager assigned to evaluate a portfolio of projects and to make recommendations to a selection authority, a decision policy helps avoid non–value adding work. Consider the following six decision policy elements:

1. A project's value will be traceable to goals of the organization and be supportive of strategy.
2. Soft costs and benefits, in accordance with the with-without principle of capital budgeting, will be used as tiebreakers between competing projects of otherwise equal hard costs and benefits.
3. Between two projects of otherwise equal value, the project that is more optimum to the financial well-being of the organization will be selected first.
4. All projects will adhere to the ethical, regulatory, and lawful constraints and policies of the organization.
5. Projects that advance the mission or respond directly to commitments made on behalf of the organization by senior authority may be selected over other projects of greater financial reward.
6. All projects will be evaluated for risk. Among projects of equal objective risk measures, those least risk-averse will be given greater priority.

Decision Tools for Selecting Projects

Decision tools for project selection fill out the decision framework. For the functional criteria, the with-without principle is a tool for obtaining an estimate of soft costs. For all costs, the three financial evaluation tools used in this book are net present value, economic value add, and expected monetary value (see Chapter 1).

UNDERSTANDING THE PROJECT BALANCE SHEET: IMPLEMENTING THE PROJECT EQUATION

Most project managers are familiar with the accountant's concept of a balance sheet: Assets, on one side, are "balanced" by liabilities and owner's equity on the other side. The sheet balances because it conforms to an equation—the accounting equation—that is stated in two forms:

> ### The Accounting Equation
> *Assets = Liabilities + Equity*
> *That owned by the company = Value made available to the company from lenders (liabilities) and investors/sponsors (equity)*

The second equation provides an analogy with projects. The balance sheet is extendable to project management as a tool for weighing the project investor/sponsor's needs on the one hand with the project manager's estimates of capability and capacity on the other.

The Project Balance Sheet Concept

Just as in the accountant's balance sheet that weighed the liabilities and equity provided by others with the capacity of the business to use its assets to produce value, that same paradigm exists in projects.[4] Consider Figure 3-2.

On the left side of the project balance sheet is the value proposition of the project. Value has been developed during strategic planning as a flow-down from opportunity into goals, and through strategy into projects. The left side arrow is shown downward to continue the top-down metaphor. Project value, expectations, and business or organizational requirements come to the project manager top-down from the enterprise. Project investors/sponsors often view the project as a "black box"; they often have little interest in the project details, the "how-to" of achieving value. They care principally that value be delivered for the agreed investment.

FIGURE 3-2   Project balance sheet balances value with capability and capacity

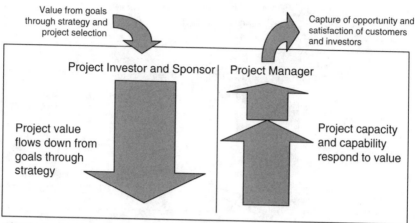

Value from goals through strategy and project selection

Capture of opportunity and satisfaction of customers and investors

Project Investor and Sponsor | Project Manager

Project value flows down from goals through strategy

Project capacity and capability respond to value

Adapted and reprinted from author's articles with permission from PMI®

On the right side of the project balance sheet the arrows are shown upward, signifying the bottoms-up approach to evaluating facts. Insofar as the facts come up short in their support for the business case, risk is taken to balance the right side with the left side. It is too harsh to say that project managers—the custodians of the right side of the balance sheet—do not care about value, but certainly their first priority is to use facts to obtain sufficient resources so that managing variances is not their main task.

The common thread that connects the left and right sides of the balance sheet is a shared understanding of scope.[5] Scope, rather than cost and schedule, is the component of the triple constraint that is understood best among the various parties involved in developing a project balance sheet and project charter. Scope is the mutually negotiated understanding that binds all parties to a project plan to create value for all concerned. Figure 3-3 illustrates the bridging effect of scope on the project balance sheet.

The Left Side of the Project Balance Sheet

The left side of the balance sheet is the business case for the project. It records the outcome of the decision selection process. The left side of the balance sheet corresponds to the investor/sponsor's contribution and allocation of resources to the project and the scope of the needs and wants that are to be satisfied in return for the investment.

FIGURE 3-3   Scope binds project balance sheet

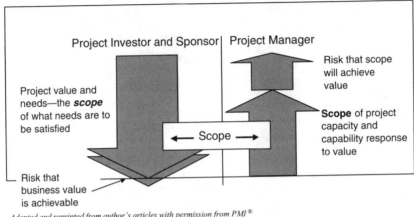

A common understanding of scope binds the left and right
side of the project balance sheet

Adapted and reprinted from author's articles with permission from PMI®

Thinking of the left side as the investor/sponsor's account (Figure 3-4), the account portfolio consists of the business case, the financial measures and imperatives, the milestones that are of value to the project investor/sponsor, and the organizational assets committed to the project.

FIGURE 3-4   Investor's and sponsor's account holds all project values

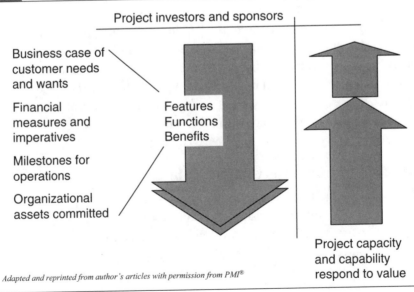

Adapted and reprinted from author's articles with permission from PMI®

The business case takes many forms, but typically it is written functionally and serves the following purposes:

- Documents the flow-down from goals and strategy, describing context and domain for customers, users, maintainers, and other stakeholders
- Provides the quantitative justification and analysis for the project
- Imparts a vision of the concept of operations after project development ends and the operational life of the deliverable begins
- Describes the necessary features for end-users
- Details the benefit plan for recovering the project's investment
- Lists or references constraints, assumptions, rules, policies, and regulations.

The Right Side of the Project Balance Sheet

Figure 3-5 details the right side of the project balance sheet, which is the project team's response to the project charter. It illustrates a common dilemma: The estimated capability and capacity of the project team are insufficient to meet all the value requirements placed on the project. The right-side estimates come from an evaluation of the "facts." Facts are developed about the work breakdown structure and statement of work required to meet the scope. Facts are developed about the cost and schedule required by the work statement. Often, the facts developed are not in agreement with the

---

FIGURE 3-5   Project account holds all project capability, capacity, and risk

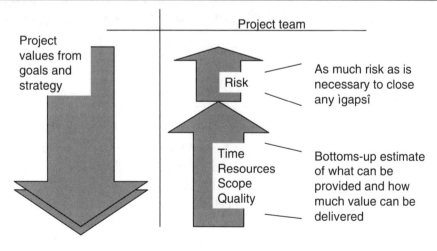

Adapted and reprinted from author's articles with permission from PMI®

---

business case. Either more money or time is required, or the scope needs to be reduced to conform to available funds and schedule.

The misalignment between the left-side business case and the facts-driven estimates creates a gap between the right and left sides of the balance sheet. To close the gap and balance the business case with the implementation demands, a balancing element is needed to achieve balance. This balancing element is risk.

The project balance sheet is negotiated between the investors/sponsors and the implementers. An objective of the implementing team is to use conservative estimates of expected value for all implementation components. Recall from Chapter 1 that expected value is the best estimator of an outcome in the face of uncertainty. Expected value requires a sample of the population of outcomes, but often this sample is as simple as three estimates for each component: a pessimistic value, an optimistic value, and the most probable value.

The negotiating objective of the project investors/sponsors is to retain as much value as possible for the available investment. In the course of negotiations, it is reasonable to expect the value expectation to decrease and the expected value of resources to increase, thereby closing the gap somewhat. Nevertheless, it is inevitable that there will be a remaining gap.

The project team must collectively accept some risk to meet all the value requirements presented on the left side. How much risk? The answer is: only as much as is required to close the gap and achieve balance. Risk, viewed this way, is derived. It is derived from the independent variables of project values flowed onto the left side and the "undeniable" facts of capacity and capability estimated on the right side.

Three categories of risk need to be managed on the project balance sheet:

1. Uncertainty regarding the estimates of cost and schedule. Chapters 5 and 6 discuss these risks in more detail.
2. Uncertainty regarding whether the value estimates to the business are correct. This is primarily a left-side risk to be managed by the "benefits manager," a position detailed in Chapter 6.
3. Uncertainty regarding how cost investments on the right side specifically yield value benefits on the left side. This risk arises from the integrated effect of the left and right sides. It is a risk that is managed actively by the project manager, but in dialogue with the project investors/sponsors who are looking forward to applying the project deliverables in the business.[6]

Resolving Balance Sheet Issues

The project manager takes the lead in resolving the balance sheet issues. The project manager employs the following traditional steps in risk management:

- Identify all material risks in each of the categories described above.
- Quantify their impact on the project, and adjust expected values accordingly.
- Develop mitigations for the calculated impacts.
- Transfer residue risk to the project balance sheet.

Figure 3-6 provides the road map to working iteratively around the balance sheet. This road map is really an iteration of several steps intended to arrive at a "negotiated" agreement with the project investors/sponsors and the project team. Working left to right on the balance sheet, the objectives in each step are as follows

- In step 1, the project manager seeks to make time an ally, deferring those requirements that can be delivered later. The project manager evaluates whether the passage of time will bring new solution possibilities or just introduce uncertainty. Either way, all future possibilities and approaches must be brought to a common baseline using expected value.

FIGURE 3-6   Road map to resolving risk in attaining value

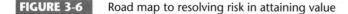

1. Lay all value requirements on a timeline
2. Identify benefit stream with each identifiable requirement
3. Reorder requirements according to benefit attainment
4. Re-time all requirements and reevaluate commitments of assets

1. For each requirement, derive risk from timeline of deliverables
2. Evaluate ways to improve benefits
3. Reorder requirements according to risk-adjusted benefit attainment, expected benefits
4. Negotiate terms and conditions to reduce risks
5. Place residual risk on the balance sheet

- In step 2, the project manager allocates benefits to requirements, seeking to identify and then eliminate all non–value-adding requirements.
- In step 3, the project manager puts a new plan in place that incorporates the results of steps 1 and 2.
- Step 4 is the wrap-up, a step that might occur after much iteration in earlier steps. In effect, all other conditions that affect capability and capacity that are not requirements-based are addressed. Items included in this step are funding schedules, facilities, tools, staff, training, availability of outside subject matter experts and contracted assistance, benefit ramp-up, and roll-out strategy.
- At step 5 there is a residual risk that has not otherwise been accommodated. This risk is the derived risk, and it goes on the balance sheet. If it does not provide a state of risk acceptance by project sponsor and project manager, then the project should not proceed.

The Project Equation and the Project Manager's Mission

It is almost self-evident that placing residual risk on the project side of the balance sheet means that it is the project manager's responsibility to manage. Therefore, the project manager's mission and the project equation are restated as shown below.

> ### Project Manager's Mission and Project Equation
>
> *The project manager's mission is to manage project resource capability and capacity to deliver expected scope, taking measured risks to do so.*
>
> *The project equation is given by: Value delivered from resources committed is equal to capability and capacity plus risks taken.*

The project equation is the "new math" for the project manager. This is the equation that must be satisfied for the project to be successful.

- A rational decision framework is needed to select projects derived from goals and strategy.
- Rational means predictable outcomes from the application of information to a process.
- A decision framework consists of decision criteria, decision tools, and a decision policy.
- The project balance sheet is a tool for balancing the triple constraints, risks, and the value expectations of project investors/sponsors. The left side of the balance sheet holds project values; the right side holds expected capability and capacity to deliver value and the residual risk to do so.
- The project manager's mission is to manage assigned resources to deliver the scope expected, taking measured risks to do so.
- The project equation is given by: Value delivered from resources committed is equal to capability and capacity plus risks taken.

NOTES

1. John C. Goodpasture and David T. Hulett, "A Balance Sheet for Projects: A Guide to Risk-Based Value, Part I and Part II," *PM Network*, May and June 2000 (Sylva, NC: Project Management Institute, 2000).
2. John D. Martin and J. William Petty, *Value Based Management* (Boston: Harvard Business School Press, 2000).
3. Robert C. Higgins, *Analysis for Financial Management* (Boston: Irwin/McGraw-Hill, 1998), p. 251.
4. John C. Goodpasture and David T. Hulett, "A Balance Sheet for Projects: A Guide to Risk-Based Value, Part I and Part II," *PM Network*, May and June 2000 (Sylva, NC: Project Management Institute, 2000).
5. Jonathan Goodwin. Insight provided to the author that the right and left sides of the project balance sheet are bound by a common understanding of scope, 2000.
6. Ibid.

CHAPTER 4

Estimating the Future

There is likely no factor that would contribute more to the success of any project than having a good and complete definition of the project's scope of work.

—QUENTIN FLEMING AND JOEL KOPPELMAN
Earned Value Project Management, 2000

There are no facts in the future. It is that simple. Only estimates of future events, tasks, activities, and outcomes can be made. Of course, the task of project managers is to deliver value to the stakeholders of their projects, and that delivery will be in the future. So, what can project managers say and do about the value those stakeholders will receive?

This chapter discusses how to plan for the future and address the risks of uncertain outcomes. First, we describe how project managers define scope, a critical first step to filling in the left side of the project balance sheet and setting expectations with project sponsors. Second, we address the issue of how project managers plan the delivery of value and accommodate changing gaps that arise in the future. Last, we discuss how to identify risks in project plans and mitigate their effects.

SCOPING THE FUTURE

From the discussion of the project balance sheet in Chapter 3, recall that the value side of the balance sheet (i.e., the left side) represents the purpose, payback objective, and scope required of the project. Typically, these elements constitute the "business case," and they are recorded in the project charter. The right side of the balance sheet is the response to the business case. It is the implementation plan for achieving the required outcomes. The right side is the project team's estimates of scope, schedule, resources, and risk.

The Project Charter and Business Case

"A project charter is a document that formally authorizes a project . . . [and includes directly or by reference]. . .the business need that the project was undertaken to address."[1] The business need is often referred to as the "business case." The business case states the business need and justifies the project in business terms. Consider this example of a business case:

> ### Business Case
>
> *The purpose of this project is make our company "easier to do business with" by improving customer satisfaction with our order entry and order management processes and procedures. Currently, customers rate the importance of our order entry system as 9 on a scale of 10, but satisfaction is rated only 5 on a scale of 10. Satisfaction means how convenient, timely, accurate, and responsive the ordering processes are. The management team is prepared to charter a project and make investments to obtain improvements in our ordering system. These improvements must achieve a satisfaction rating of 9 on a scale of 10 and earn positive present value economic value add (PV EVA) over the first three years of operations.*

This business case has the following characteristics: it is solution-free; it states a timeframe (a basis for accepting a project proposal in response to this business need); and it provides quantitative measures of value. The project manager understands from this business case that the project is valuable if, after delivery and roll-out: (1) customers are sufficiently satisfied that they will rate the order entry system as a 9 on a scale of 10 for functionality and capacity, and (2) the project is a financial success, as measured by positive EVA over the first three years of operations.

Often, the business case incorporates business rules. Business rules are not requirements per se, but rather they are constraints, policies, procedures, or limits and boundaries that apply to the project. Project managers may be required to apply, enforce, and report about compliance to business rules. In the business case example given above, the business rules are not stated directly, but the following business rules might apply:

- Projects accepted for implementation must have positive PV EVA.
- For "customer-facing" projects, as this one is, the measure of success from the perspective of the business is in the hands of the customer.
- Three years of operation are used for financial benefits measurement.

The business case in context with the business rules is the baseline for the value side of the balance sheet. This is the first value baseline for the project, labeled "Value Baseline 1.0."

Requirements Translation

To scope the future, the business case must be translated into requirements. Requirements are statements of capacity and capability that affect project stakeholders. Capacity is viewed as addressing fitness to time and space (space in three dimensions); capability is thought of as function and process provided by the project. Kulak and Guiney state: "A requirement is something that [a deliverable] must do for its users. It is a specific function or feature or principle that the [deliverable] must provide in order for it to merit existence. Requirements constitute the scope of the [project]. Add a few requirements, and the scope increases; take some away, and the scope decreases."[2]

Translation of the value statements in the business case into actionable implementation requirements is necessary before the right side of the balance sheet can be quantified. The requirements translation process is often represented by the "V-model," illustrated in Figure 4-1. In the V-model,

FIGURE 4-1   V-model illustrates the requirements process

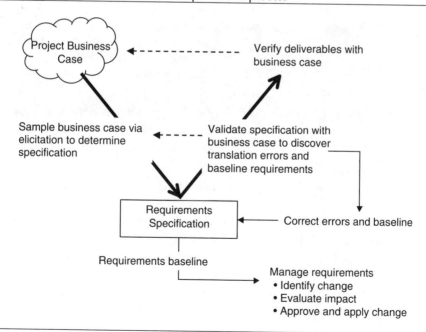

the project investor/sponsor's statement of need, as expressed in the project charter and business case, is at the top left of the V. At the bottom of the V is the requirements specification. In between is the process of translation.

Translation is a sampling process. The term "sample" is used in the sense of completeness. Only a finite amount of information contained in the "ideas" of the business case are translated by interview, analysis, or trial into the specification. Other information is latent and not revealed; therefore, it is not in the sample or, as is the nature of sampling, some detail may be inadequately represented.

Project managers familiar with risk management recognize the dilemma: No matter how diligent and detailed the effort applied to the task of writing the requirement, the written document is but a sampling of the business idea. Unavoidably, there is some sampling error. This sampling error is the first source of risk for the right side of the balance sheet.

Consider the illustrative business case and responding requirement that follow.[3]

Business Case

Our wireless telephone service will be implementing "less-than-one-minute rating" billing for national and international long distance wireline and cellular usage as of the next calendar year in order to remain competitive with industry trends. Although there may be a direct reduction in revenue, overall the impact on customer satisfaction will more than offset revenue losses.

Requirement

Less-than-one-minute ratings: A billing capability for less-than-one-minute ratings shall be implemented for (a) national and (b) international long distance calls originated from wireline access and by means of cellular calls. This billing capability shall be operational for business beginning on [date]. It shall bill according to rate tables to be adjusted for competitive advantage on a periodic basis.

Is there sampling error between the idea and the requirement? Has every idea embodied in the business case been accounted for in the requirement? Certainly the business need to stay in front of the competition and not suffer too much revenue loss is explicit in the business case but not directly represented in the requirement. There are likely many functional ramifications to changing a business process that are not directly stated. This business case–requirements pair is representative of the problems inherent in requirements translation.

The validation and verification steps are located on the right side of the V, proceeding upward from the specification (see Figure 4-1). Validation is a step performed before implementation of deliverables. Validation confirms that the specification is an adequate representation of the business idea. In effect, validation confirms that the "sampling error" is negligibly small. Verification is done after deliverable implementation and "proves" that the deliverable is as specified and as required in the business case. In the example given for the wireless service provider, the errors discovered during validation would likely be about call origination methods, minimum billing charges, and internal reporting on call metrics and revenue metrics by service offering.

The topic of validation and verification is too extensive to be covered in detail in this book. Table 4-1 presents the primary methods for each.

PLANNING THE DELIVERY OF VALUE

For any number of reasons, it is often necessary to spread the satisfaction of requirements over a period of time. This process is called "sequencing." Sequencing may be explicitly required by the business case, or it may be a consequence of requirements translation and project planning. Typically several requirements are grouped together for delivery at some scheduled date. Each such grouping is called a "requirements group" or "release" to distinguish such a grouping from the term "deliverables." Deliverables are outcomes of packages of work in the project work breakdown structure. Many deliverables, or only one deliverable, may be contained within a

TABLE 4-1 Validation and Verification Methods

	Method	Comment
Validation	Requirements analysis	Accomplished by independent validation team consisting of subject matter experts
	Modeling and simulation	Models or simulates performance of deliverable meeting requirements; requires that model or simulation be independently verified for accuracy
Verification	Test	Measurement of actual performance of deliverables
	Demonstration	Actual performance of deliverable functions
	Analysis	Calculation of deliverable performance where actual performance cannot be measured; useful as alternative to destructive testing
	Inspection	Observance of deliverable characteristics without quantitative measurements; applies to many quality requirements

requirements group. As shown in Figure 4-2, the business value of the project accumulates over time as requirements groups become operational.

The requirements specification and the sequenced requirements groups become the requirements baseline for the implementation side of the balance sheet. It is labeled "Requirements Baseline 1," and the requirement groups are numbered from 1 to N for this baseline.

Table 4-2 shows the project balance sheet after the baselining of the business case and the translation of the business case into a set of requirements specifications with requirement groups.

Choosing between Implementation Alternatives

Once requirements are baselined, at least at a functional and performance level sufficient to determine how the project benefits will be achieved, it is

FIGURE 4-2   Requirements are satisfied in sequence

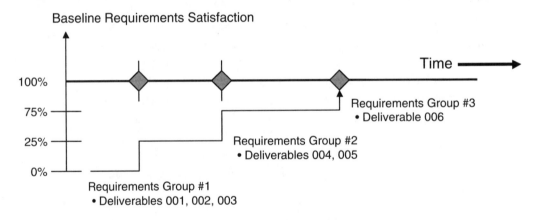

Adapted and reprinted from author's articles with permission from PMI®

TABLE 4-2   Project Balance Sheet Baseline 1

Project Value	Project Implementation
Vision state 1: Describes the state of the organization when the business case is satisfied	**Risk** from requirements translation error
Business case baseline 1: Specifies the required benefits, scope of functionality and performance, resource input, and timeline for performance and payback	**Requirements baseline 1**, as translated from the business case into an actionable requirements specification
Business rules: Specify the context, constraints, and imposed rules that govern the project	**Requirement groups 1 to N** sequence the satisfaction of the business case

time to choose an implementation alternative. The project's decision policy, decision criteria, and the tools and methods for arriving at an objective implementation decision come into play. Depending on the complexity and sophistication of the requirements, developing and understanding one or more ways to implement the requirements may require analysis, modeling, simulation, or prototyping. Once an approach is selected, the project team can refine resource, scope, and time estimates.

Decision Tables for Implementation Alternatives

When project estimates are being made, two or more alternative implementations, each with a different cost and schedule, often are available that could satisfy the value side of the balance sheet. For a variety of reasons, the decision about which to employ in the project needs to be made sometime in the future. Nevertheless, a value needs to be placed on this decision in order to complete the project balance sheet estimates. In this situation, decision trees or decision tables are used to calculate an expected value of time and resources.

Consider the example presented in Table 4-3, which shows two alternatives. The project team estimates that building deliverable XX is a little more probable than buying it, but this make-buy decision will not be made until later in the project schedule. Each alternative has a different face value of cost. The expected value of each alternative is evaluated separately before summing the results.

The total expected value is the figure that is carried to the project balance sheet as an implementation estimate for deliverable XX. The expected value becomes the budgeted cost for this item. The range of possible costs associated with this expected value provides information that can be used to estimate budget variance. Variance, used in this context, means the statistical measure of spread or distance around the expected value. This cost range is shown on the balance sheet in the risk section on the right side.

TABLE 4-3 Decision Table

Alternative ID	Description	Probability of Choosing Alternative	Face Value of Alternative	Expected Value of Deliverable XX
001	Build deliverable XX	0.6	$300K	$180K
002	Buy deliverable XX	0.4	$100K	$40K
		Total expected value for deliverable XX		$220K
	Uncertainty associated with future decision about how to acquire deliverable XX			+$80K/–$120K

Notice that the downside risk in this example is $80K. If the project manager is not averse to this downside, as may well be the case if the risk is diversified by the presence of many deliverables, each with some positive and negative uncertainty, then $80K may not be too worrisome. However, if an $80K downside exceeds the project manager's limit of acceptable risk (as discussed in Chapter 1), then the scenario in Table 4-3 may lead the project manager to consider other acquisition strategies for deliverable XX. Table 4-4 presents a balance sheet for this project.

Of course, the project investor/sponsor may not agree to the budget for the expected value of the cost of deliverable XX, and the investor/sponsor may be averse to the identified risks. Negotiations with the project manager may ensue. Some modifications to the project plan may be required to complete the approval cycle with the project manager. Some additional risk may have to be taken to close the differences between the investor/sponsor and the project team, but only as much risk as is needed to close the differences. These risks would be entered onto the balance sheet on the right side and labeled as implementation risks.

Triple Constraint Estimates on the Balance Sheet

To complete the project balance sheet, the project manager adds the triple constraint estimates to the balance sheet, building on the work already done on the initial baseline and illustrated in Table 4-2. The project manager also adds the risk representing the uncertainty faced in all projects that the requirements might change during the course of the project. Table 4-5 presents the completed project balance sheet.

Gap Analysis

Project managers are all too aware that nothing remains constant over the lifecycle of a project. As strategic planning occurs periodically, or as the project investors/sponsors become aware of changes in customers, markets,

---

TABLE 4-4 Project Balance Sheet for Deliverable XX

Project Value	Project Implementation
Business case baseline 1: Provide deliverable XX to the business by [date]	**Make-buy risk:** +$80K/–$120K
	Requirements baseline 1: Deliverable XX is to be acquired after make-buy analysis for an expected value cost of $220K **Requirement groups 1:** Deliverable XX

TABLE 4-5 Project Balance Sheet

Project Value	Project Implementation
Vision state 1: of the organizatic case is satisfied	translation error between business case and
Business case b the required bene functionality and resource input, ar performance and	between resources offered in the business tion estimates y that requirements may change during the
Business rules: constraints, and in govern the project	e 1, as translated from the business case into nts specification 1 to N sequence the satisfaction of the nates of scope, resources, and time

(handwritten notes: wk 3, 07/28, Goodpasture 4, verzuh 9)

competition, tec   tions, and labor and
raw material av   these will affect the
"vision" of wher   er all, "The essential
undertaking of b   tually been for many
years: Understan   value."[4]

As customer   ponse must change. Accordingly, dur   ion, there may be a change in vision   vision is less precise and more expans   iirements, creating a gap that has an ex

Although bus   areness and observa-
tion of the firm's   the project vision is
fixed in one state   hange, often abrupt,
is one of many cha   roject manager. Each change in the vision brings a change in value and benefits expected of the project.

Figure 4-3 illustrates a step-wise change in vision from baseline state 1 to subsequent states. Notice the offset between the vision states and the requirements baseline. This offset is called the "vision gap." Subsequently, when a change in vision state is "approved" by the change management process, the project manager immediately sees that the "requirements gap" between the requirements groups and the vision baseline is now changed as well. In effect, the requirements are now "chasing the vision." To evaluate

FIGURE 4-3 Vision gaps arise from change in vision state

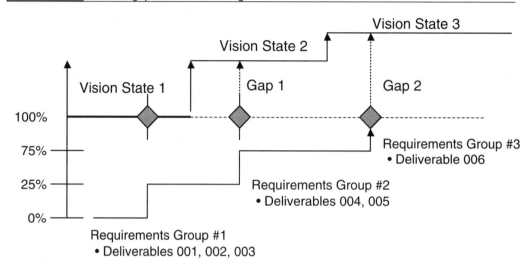

Adapted and reprinted from author's articles with permission from PMI ®

the requirements gap, the project manager assesses impacts to requirements caused by a change in the state of the vision. From this assessment, requirements impacts are submitted for change management approval, thereby creating a new requirements baseline.

Table 4-6 illustrates the new project balance sheet created as a consequence of a change in vision state.

TABLE 4-6 Project Balance Sheet Baseline Change

Project Value	Project Implementation
Vision state 2: A modified vision state for the organization	**Risk** from original baseline
	Risk added from impacts due to change in vision state
Business case baseline 2: Baseline 1 plus changes from baseline 1 in benefits, scope, resources, and timeline, as aligned with the new vision state	**Requirements baseline 2**, as translated from the changed business case into a modified requirements specification
Business rules: Change, as appropriate	**Requirement groups 1 to N**, which sequence the satisfaction of the business case

EVALUATING RISKS ON THE PROJECT BALANCE SHEET

On the project balance sheet, there are three risk categories on the right side:

1. The risk from translation errors that arise from developing and specifying functional and performance requirements from the business case
2. The risk from uncertainty in implementation due to design, development, and test of "make" items or uncertainty in vendor performance for "buy" items
3. The risk arising from changes to requirements not anticipated by the project manager.

On the left side, there is the risk that the business value will not materialize even if the implementation is a success. There also is some uncertainty that each marginal dollar of investment is going to yield some proportional marginal increase in value. This latter uncertainty is sometimes labeled "gold plate," referring to added cost that may not translate into added value.

These risks need to be evaluated in quantitative terms for the project balance sheet. Chapter 11 of *A Guide to the Project Management Body of Knowledge* contains a good overview of risk evaluation.

Risk Evaluation

Risk is the word used for uncertainty of outcome. Given that the goal here is numbers that can be transferred to the project balance sheet, the emphasis is on quantitative risk analysis. Chapter 1 introduced the concept of expected value and defined it as "outcome times the probability that the outcome will occur." This relationship can be expressed as follows:

$$\text{Expected value} = \sum x_i * p_i$$

where the sum is made over all values of i, x_i is the i'th nondeterministic outcome, p_i is the probability that the i'th outcome will occur, and $\sum p_i = 1$. Recall from the previous discussion that the expected value is an unbiased maximum likelihood estimator for the true mean value, μ, of the population of x_i.

Consider the following example.

Expected Value

A project manager may need to buy a special tool. If it becomes necessary, the cost is $10K; otherwise the cost equals $0. There are two x_i values:

$10K and $0. The project manager estimates that the probability of buying the tool is 0.7; if so, then the probability of not buying the tool is 0.3. The expected value of the tool purchase is calculated as: 0.7 × $10K + 0.3 × $0 = $7K. The downside risk is $3K.

Now, an outcome of $7K cannot actually occur; only a $10K or $0 can really happen. However, in the face of the uncertainty as to which will occur, the project manager's "best" single point estimator for the budget for this tool is $7K.

To evaluate risks for the balance sheet, the project manager needs the following data:

- An identification and label for each risk event or circumstance
- A description of each identified risk
- An estimate of the impact on the project for outcomes that might happen if the risk event or circumstance were to occur
- An estimate of the probability for each identified outcome
- A calculation of the expected impact on the project
- A decision policy that provides guidance regarding objective risk decisions and risk-averse decisions

With this information in hand, the project manager can complete a table of risk quantification. Table 4-7 presents an example.

Statistical Distributions for the Project Balance Sheet

The project manager refines figures in the risk quantification table or the decision table by employing statistical distributions. Statistical distributions describe a range of uncertainty rather than a point estimate and a probability. Working from experience, the project manager assumes an applicable probability distribution for each of the outcomes and for the distribution, and makes an estimate of the governing parameters.

Many distributions could be employed. However, project managers commonly use three distributions because of their applicability to a wide range of real situations. Table 4-8 and Figure 4-4 explain these distributions.

Figure 4-5 illustrates the results of using these distributions on a set of estimates.

TABLE 4-7 Risk Quantification Example for the Project Balance Sheet

Risk ID	Description	Outcome	Probability That the Outcome Will Occur	Expected Monetary Value to Be Recorded on the Project Balance Sheet	
				Cost Consequence of Delay: $5K per Delay Day	
001	Translation error in functionality XX	45-day schedule impact	0.3	13.5 days	$67.5K
		0-day schedule impact	0.7	0 days	$0K
002	Vision state translation error of functionality YY	21-day schedule impact	0.5	10.5 days	$52.5K
		0-day schedule impact	0.5	0 days	$0K
003	Implementation cost estimate uncertainty	$500K over	0.2	N/A	$100K
		–$70K under	0.8	N/A	–$56K
004	Implementation schedule estimate uncertainty	60 days late	0.4	24 days	$120K
		–10 days early	0.6	–6 days	–$30K

N/A—not applicable.

TABLE 4-8 Statistical Distributions for Cost and Schedule Estimates

Distribution	Application	Key Statistics
Normal	Applies to naturally occurring phenomenon where there are equally likely outcomes above and below a mean value	Mean and standard deviation
		The most pessimistic (p) or optimistic (o) values are estimated as being *approximately* ± three standard deviations, σ, from the mean.
		The variance, σ^2, is then *approximated* by the following formula: $[(o - p)/6]^2$.
		The mean and most likely values, which are at the peak of the bell curve, are equal.
Beta	Applies to naturally occurring phenomenon where there is a high probability that outcomes will be skewed either above or below a "most likely" outcome	Most likely value (m), most pessimistic (p), most optimistic (o), and mean value
		The most likely value is the value around which most outcomes cluster. The mean is *approximated* by the formula: $(p + o + 4m)/6$.
		The variance, σ^2, is then approximated by the following formula: $[(o - p)/6]^2$. It is the same formula used for the approximation of the normal distribution.
		The mean value is different from the most likely value.
Triangular	Same as beta, except triangular is a model of the beta used to simplify the mathematics	Mean value is calculated as: $[o + m + p]/3$.
		Variance is calculated using the following formula: $[(o - p)^2 + (m - o)(m - p)]/18$.

FIGURE 4-4   Probability distributions for risk analysis

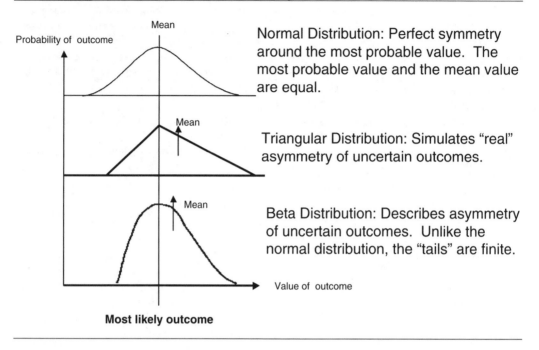

Normal Distribution: Perfect symmetry around the most probable value. The most probable value and the mean value are equal.

Triangular Distribution: Simulates "real" asymmetry of uncertain outcomes.

Beta Distribution: Describes asymmetry of uncertain outcomes. Unlike the normal distribution, the "tails" are finite.

FIGURE 4-5   Applying probability distributions to project estimates

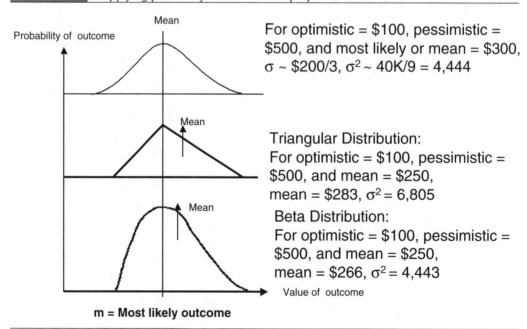

For optimistic = $100, pessimistic = $500, and most likely or mean = $300, $\sigma \sim \$200/3$, $\sigma^2 \sim 40K/9 = 4{,}444$

Triangular Distribution:
For optimistic = $100, pessimistic = $500, and mean = $250,
mean = $283, $\sigma^2 = 6{,}805$

Beta Distribution:
For optimistic = $100, pessimistic = $500, and mean = $250,
mean = $266, $\sigma^2 = 4{,}443$

- The project business case and business rules are captured on the value side of the project balance sheet.
- The V-model expresses the requirements translation process and identifies the source of translation error risks.
- The project manager's implementation side of the project balance sheet has three major risks: (1) translation errors, (2) implementation cost and schedule estimate errors, and (3) changing requirements.
- Satisfying the business case by a timed roll-out of deliverables creates a requirements gap until all deliverables have been completed.
- Changes in vision state during the lifecycle of the project can lead to additional risks and create gaps between the vision and the ability of the project team to deliver.
- Risk on the project balance sheet is evaluated using expected value methods.
- Decision tables and statistical distributions add refinement to the calculation of expected value.
- The most commonly employed distributions in estimating cost and schedule are the normal, beta, and triangular distributions.

NOTES

1. *A Guide to the Project Management Body of Knowledge, 2000 Edition* (Upper Darby, PA: Project Management Institute, 2000), p. 54.
2. Daryl Kulak and Eamonn Guiney, *Uses Cases Requirements in Context* (New York: Addison-Wesley, 2000), p. 4.
3. John C. Goodpasture. This example is derived from material developed by the author for the training course "How to Capture Requirements and Develop Project Scope," available from Catalyst Management Consulting, LLC, Findlay, OH, 2000.
4. James C. Anderson and James A. Narus, *Business Market Management: Understanding, Creating, and Delivering Value* (Upper Saddle River, NJ: Prentice Hall, 1999).

CHAPTER 5

Delivering Value

Performance measurement is an essential part of management control in that it validates whether the results anticipated from planned action are realized.

—Kiran Verma
Total Factor Productivity Management, 1992

I n the final analysis, projects are chartered to deliver value to the business and its stakeholders. Successful achievement of business value depends on measuring progress along the way. The two basic categories of measurements are:

1. **Earned value.** This category addresses how well implementation resources are being employed to acquire and make operational the outcomes of the project in the timeframe desired. This measurement is about progressive project accomplishment according to a baseline plan. Earned value systems have been around a long time, going by many different names; they have been a part of project management since the 1960s.[1]

2. **Value attainment.** This category addresses how well the deliverables are being employed operationally to achieve the benefits and returns in the business case. Achievement of business goals may require measurements to be made throughout the lifecycle of the endeavor from project implementation through deliverables retirement and salvage. The name sometimes given to the aggregate of an implementation project and its follow-on operations and salvage is "program."

Project manager success is usually measured by the first metric, earned value, because the charter to the implementation project usually limits the project manager's responsibility and authority. Yet the project itself may well be measured by value attainment. Although attainment of organizational benefits and returns is often beyond the timeframe of the implementation project, and attainment of these benefits is itself not a project task, the fact remains that for many projects the judgment on success will be based less on implementation performance and more on operational effectiveness of what the project provides.

One need only look to some spectacular operational misses (e.g., New Coke® or the Edsel automobile) to see that project implementation success is often a small achievement compared with operational success, or not. Accordingly, there is a requirement for a "benefits manager" to be the responsible party for value attainment and benefits achievement (see Figure 5-1).

EARNED VALUE

Value does not happen all at once; it builds up over time. The project lifecycle bounds the timeframe for project value and benefits measurements. The three phases in the lifecycle, as shown in Figure 5-2, are:

1. **Initiating and conceptualizing.** In this phase, the project is conceived during the process of goal deployment and strategic planning, as described in Chapter 2. The business case is written, and the project is chartered.

2. **Implementation.** The project balance sheet is baselined, and a project plan for project execution is written and approved. The project team executes the project to a successful closeout of the implementation.

FIGURE 5-1   Value measures change during project lifecycle

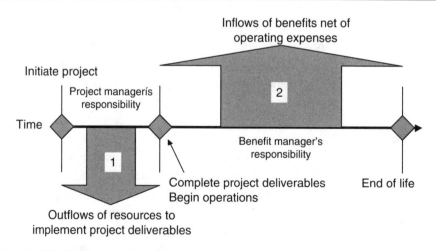

FIGURE 5-2   Value is accumulated throughout the project lifecycle

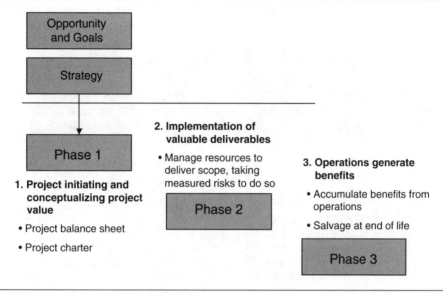

3. **Operations, salvage, and disposal.** The deliverables are applied operationally to earn benefits, used to the end of their life, and then retired. If the deliverables are sold to external customers, this third phase may consist of post-sale support to those customers.

ACCOMPLISHING PROJECT TASKS TO EARN VALUE

Value accumulation during implementation is measured by a metric called earned value. "Value attainment" is the term coined for value accumulation during operations after completion of project implementation. Value attainment is the subject of Chapter 6.

To earn value, it is not enough to apply activity to tasks in the work scope. In fact, activity--no matter how extensive at whatever cost—may not earn any value. Only accomplishment of scope earns value. Therefore, the project manager focuses on accomplishment.

The project is the sum of its tasks; therefore, each task contributes in part to the delivery of value. Project tasks are defined during project scheduling. Scheduling begins after the business case or project scope is organized into a work breakdown structure (WBS). Each package of work in the WBS is then decomposed by means of task planning into the various work activities. Total satisfaction of the value proposition requires completing all of the scope contained within the work packages. Recall from earlier discussions that the totality of scope may be planned as several delivery releases extending over some period of time.

> ### *Value Delivery*
>
> *Delivering all the value means delivering all the scope within an expenditure of time and resources that is equal to or less than the planned and baselined amounts.*

Scope, time, and resources form the project triple constraint. Recall that the triple constraint, as illustrated by the triangle in Figure 5-3, is itself a functional equation of independent and dependent variables of the form expressed by the following equation:

$$z = f(x, y)$$

One leg of the triangle, x, is usually made a high priority and planned for certain accomplishment. The second leg, y, is optimized for accomplishment after x is planned or estimated. The third leg, z, is derived from the function of x and y; z is derived and takes on whatever value is necessary to close the triple constraint.

FIGURE 5-3 The triple constraint relates scope, schedule, and cost

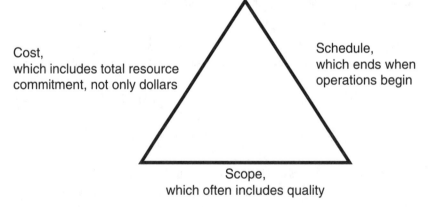

Cost, which includes total resource commitment, not only dollars

Schedule, which ends when operations begin

Scope, which often includes quality

Changing one side affects at least one other side.
In the triple constraint, fix the size of the most important side, optimize the next most important side, and the size of the third side is dependent on the other two.

Consider the example below.

> ### *Example*
>
> The **scope** *of the project (x) is to build a residential three-bedroom house. The* **schedule** *(y) is to complete construction and obtain a certificate of occupancy within 150 days from contract beginning. The dependent variable (z) is* **cost***, which is a function of scope and schedule. The risk of achievement of the scope in the allowed timeframe is covered by a "risk premium" added to the cost. If a schedule problem arises, money may have to be spent to solve it. The buyer has made the value decision that schedule has a higher priority than cost. In other words, schedule is a more beneficial value than cost to the buyer.*

COST-CENTRIC EARNED VALUE SYSTEMS

"The purpose of earned value is to measure accomplishment and predict outcome . . . using units of measure at the core of the value system for the project."[2] To have an earned value system and make it operate properly, the following essentials[3] are required:

- **The scope for the project is fully defined.** The defined scope is really the only scope to which the project manager can apply a value earning system. In many cases, the full scope of the project may not be well defined, thereby requiring "rolling wave planning" to refine the scope over time. Chapter 4 discussed the concept of phased release of deliverables to achieve the project goals over a span of time. These phases may not be fully defined at the outset, but become defined as each wave of planning occurs.

- **A bottoms-up baseline plan for the work to be accomplished exists.** The project manager and the project team develop this plan as part of the balance sheet estimating effort. This plan identifies each package of work, organizes these packages into a WBS, and assigns resources to each package of work. The totality of all the work in the WBS should accomplish all the scope.

- **There is a timeframe for the work to be accomplished.** The timeframe is a matter of scheduling. Scheduling takes into account dependencies among tasks in the work package and dependencies with other tasks in the project, resource availability, other constraints, and the duration of the tasks in the work package.

Defining the Work to Be Accomplished

Project work is organized into a hierarchical tree structure called the WBS. Figure 5-4 depicts a WBS. Each package of work in the WBS is defined by a profile, in effect a dictionary, consisting of the items in Table 5-1.

FIGURE 5-4   Work breakdown structure organizes all the scope

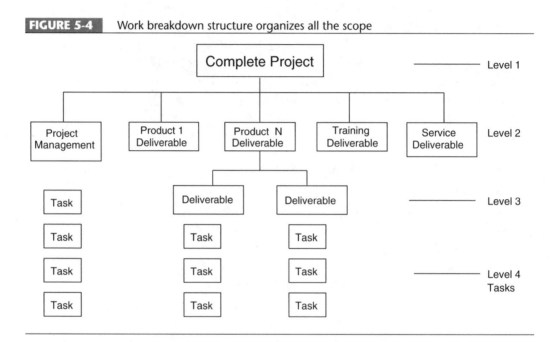

TABLE 5-1   WBS Work Package Profile or Dictionary

Item	Definition
Name	Narrative identification of the work package
ID	Identification number for the work package, typically a numerical label that reflects the WBS hierarchy (i.e., ID 1.2.2 is a third-level WBS work package subordinate to 1.2, which in turn is subordinate to 1.0)
Scope	Narrative description of the work to be performed and the deliverable of the work
Resources	Labor hours, materials, facilities, tools, and budget assigned to the work package
Rules	Constraints, standards, policies, and procedures that are applied to the work package
Schedule	The start and stop times for the work package; if not otherwise specified in the schedule, or the duration of calendar time, taken from the project schedule
Dependencies	Other tasks, internal or external, that have a direct relationship, start or finish, with this package of work
Tasks	The tasks from the lowest level of the project schedule that are accomplished as part of this package of work

Defining Earned Value Measurements

Several measures have been defined for earned value measurements over the past few decades. The latest effort produced the formal criteria issued in 1998 by the American National Standards Institute (ANSI) jointly with the Electronic Industries Association (EIA) as ANSI/EIA 748 Guide.[4] The basic measures for the guide are presented in Table 5-2.

Applying Earned Value Measurements

A simple model demonstrates how these measurements are used.[5] Figure 5-5 is an illustration of a two-task project consisting of tasks leading to Outcome A and Outcome B. Outcome A has a planned value of $10K; Outcome B has a planned value of $15K. The total work package has a planned value of $25K. At the end of the reporting period, the work package manager makes a claim of performance in order to get credit for value earned.

The project manager has some discretion about the rules governing performance claims, but these rules need to be clearly articulated before work begins. The rules address the attributes of a performance claim. Table 5-3 illustrates typical earned value rules.

In this two-outcome example, the "total credit rule" is in effect. If at the end of the reporting period, a claim of performance is made and validated such that the project manager finds only Outcome A is ready and deliverable, then the project manager must report that only $10K of value has been

TABLE 5-2   Earned Value Measurements

Measure	Definition
Planned value	The value of the work to be performed in the measurement period; formerly called the budgeted cost of work scheduled (BCWS)
Earned value	The value of the work actually accomplished, whether planned to be accomplished or not; formerly called the budgeted cost of work performed (BCWP)
Actual cost of work performed (ACWP)	The total costs actually incurred in the reporting period for the work performed in the reporting period; the ACWP includes not only the work planned to be done in the reporting period, but also all other work done but not planned
Cost performance index (CPI)	The ratio of earned value to actual cost; an efficiency measure in the sense that it measures how effective each dollar of actual cost is employed to create $1 of earned value
Schedule performance index (SPI)	The ratio of earned value to planned value; an efficiency measure on schedule in the sense that it measures how effective each dollar of planned work is being accomplished in the baseline timeframe to generate $1 of earned value

FIGURE 5-5   Two-task earned value

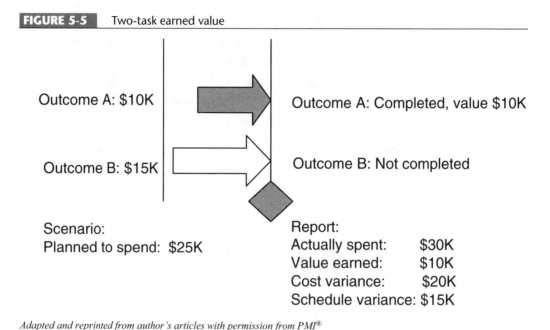

Outcome A: $10K	Outcome A: Completed, value $10K
Outcome B: $15K	Outcome B: Not completed

Scenario:
Planned to spend: $25K

Report:
Actually spent: $30K
Value earned: $10K
Cost variance: $20K
Schedule variance: $15K

Adapted and reprinted from author's articles with permission from PMI®

TABLE 5-3   Earned Value Rules

Total earned value credit only	A task is either completed fully or not. Value is earned only for a completed task; no value is earned for an incomplete task.
Partial earned value credit	Value is earned proportional to work accomplished, even though the task may not be complete. Usually, discrete partial accomplishments are specified; otherwise, this rule degenerates to "% complete," which is more often than not subjective rather than objective.
Complete means. . .	Complete means that all successor tasks can begin. If the task is an ending milestone, then closeout can begin. Typically, no more charges will be expensed to a complete work package.

earned in this report period. From the data provided in the example, $30K has been spent in the reporting period. What variances are reported? What are the expectations for completion? The project manager's report to the project investor/sponsor is shown in Table 5-4.

From this table, the project manager realizes that the efficiency of actual dollars is relatively poor: only $10/$30 = $0.33 of each actual dollar is turning into deliverable value. This ratio is called the cost performance index (CPI). The project manager forecasts the cost at completion to be: Cost of work accomplished + Value of remaining work/CPI.

TABLE 5-4	Earned Value Report to Project Investors/Sponsors ($000)						
			Report Period 1				
Value of Work Planned	**Planned Work Finished (%)**	**Value Attained**	**Cost of Work Finished**	**Value-Cost Variance**	**Schedule Variance**	**Cost at Completion**	
$25	40	$10 for A ($15 for B not attained)	$30	($20) $30 paid for $10 value	($15K) B not attained	$30 + ($15 × 30)/10 = $75	

The effectiveness of time also is poor. The schedule performance index (SPI) is similarly calculated as the ratio of value attained to value of work planned, or SPI = 10/25 = 0.4. This means that 60 percent of scheduled work—$15K—was not completed. From this index, the project manager forecasts that the remaining schedule will be 1/SPI, or 2.5 times as long as planned.

Provided that every work package can be defined according to the profile suggested, and provided that there is a measurement system for tabulating the results, the cost-centric earned value system is elegant and robust. It is predictive in the sense that if nothing changes and the reasons for performance—good or bad—repeat in the future, then past performance is a predictor of the future. However, these very predictions stimulate changes in project behavior. In other words, the impact of the earned value analysis is to mobilize actions to defeat the prediction. This in itself is a compelling reason to employ these earned value measures.[6]

A More Complex Earned Value Example

How does the project manager evaluate value earned on an additional task, especially if the task is not planned for this work period? Figure 5-6 presents this scenario.

Imagine that there was an Outcome C not planned for this reporting period, but in fact work is done on Outcome C in this reporting period. Suppose the $20K cost variance reported in Table 5-4 occurred because $15K went toward Outcome C and $5K was an overrun on Outcome A. Further suppose that Outcome C has a planned value of $30K in the second reporting period. This means that the $20K of effort toward Outcome C in period 1 did not complete Outcome C; it will be completed in the second report period. Assume that Outcome B also will be completed in the second report period. Table 5-5 provides the project manager's report of this situation.

FIGURE 5-6 Tasks are not always completed when planned

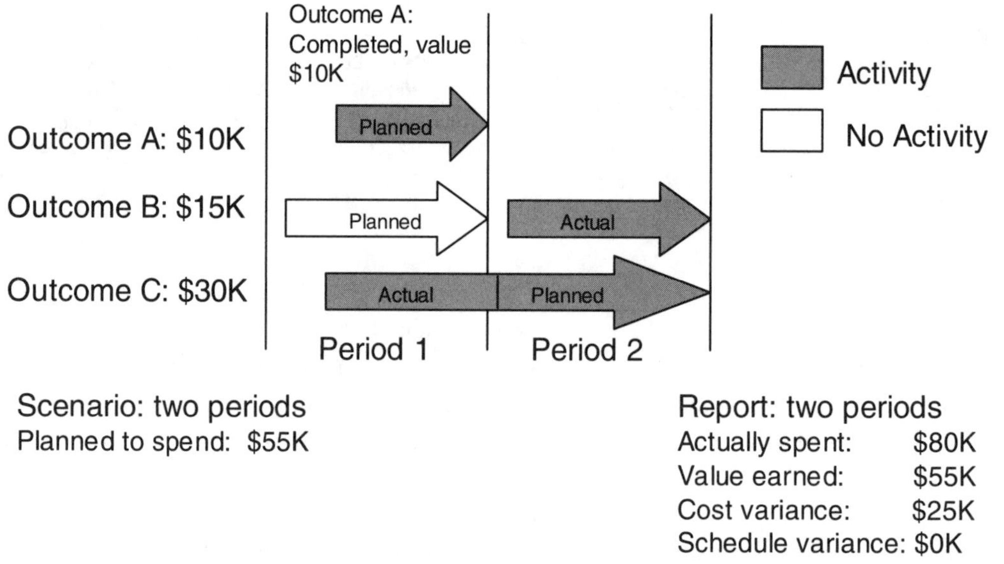

Scenario: two periods
Planned to spend: $55K

Report: two periods
Actually spent: $80K
Value earned: $55K
Cost variance: $25K
Schedule variance: $0K

Adapted and reprinted from author's articles with permission from PMI ®

TABLE 5-5 Value Earning Report to Project Sponsors ($000)

			Report Period 1			
Value of Work Planned	% of Planned Work Finished	Value Attained	Cost of Work Finished	Value-Cost Variance	Schedule Variance	Cost at Completion
$25 (A and B)	40	$10 (A but not B, $15 not attained)	$30 $15K on A $15K on C	($20)	($15) No B	$30 + [($15 + $30) × 30]/10 = $165
			Report Period 2			
$30 (C)	100	$45 (B and C)	$50 $25K on B $25K on C	($5)	0	$80

From the data provided in this table for the first reporting period, the project manager was forecasting a very large overrun of the budget. Recall that the total budget for A + B + C is $10K + $15K + $30K = $55K. In the period 1 report, the forecasted cost at completion, $165K, is $110K over the baseline. However, some recovery is made in the second period: the $15K of cost for Outcome C in period 1 not recovered with value is indeed recovered in period 2. The efficiency of the project team to obtain value from cost also is improved. The overrun is reduced to a total of $80K – $55K = $25K over plan.

Since all the measurements are linear equations, forecasting can be "worked backward." That is, if a condition is imposed top-down, then the project manager can solve an array of linear equations to determine the performance that "would have to be" in order to hit the imposed constraints. The following shows how solving linear equations might work for the example in Table 5-5 if the project sponsor insists that the $55K budget not be overrun. To begin, in the first period, the project manager needs to compute a "value/cost" index that will hold the cost at completion to $55K and then find a way to successfully apply that index to the project in the second period. The value/cost index is calculated this way:

Cost at completion = Actual cost to date + Value remaining × Cost/Value

Solving for value/cost:

$$\text{Value/Cost} = \text{(Value remaining)/} $$
$$\text{(Cost at completion} - \text{Actual cost to date)}$$

Filling in the known numbers as of the period 1 report from Table 5-5 yields the following:

$$\text{Value/Cost} = (\$15\text{K Remaining for Outcome B} + $$
$$\$15\text{K Remaining on Outcome C)/(\$55K} - \$50\text{K)} = 6.0$$

The project manager has a daunting task to improve the value/cost index to 6.0. At the end of the period 1, the value/cost index was 10/30. If partial credit is given for the work on Outcome C, this ratio improves to 25/30.

Practical Problems

Unfortunately, outside of very large organizations and organizations that are sponsored by the federal government, few organizations have adopted this cost-centric earned value system. There are many reasons, but typically there is no labor and expense cost accumulation system to drive the metrics. Few organizations use timecards for their professional workforce; many organizations do not separate operating and project expenses, and some companies cannot extend their financial ledger to pick up project expenses.

What is therefore reported? For financial measures, the project manager typically reports planned value in comparison to actual costs. Note that this is an activity measure, not a value measure, since the actual value earned is not in the equation. In lay terms, this is "budget versus actual expenditures." It is a measure of cash flow. In the example illustrated in Table 5-4, the variance would have been reported as ($5K) instead of ($20K), a considerable difference and an altogether different impression of project progress: 20 percent over budget versus 60 percent behind schedule and 80 percent over budget.

TIME-CENTRIC EARNED VALUE SYSTEMS

In 1997, the author and his project management associate James R. Sumara developed a time-centric approach to earned value[7] wherein value is associated with task starts and finishes. When a task begins or ends, value is earned. Thus, the value attached to a work period is not the dollar value of the work but rather the number of starts or finishes that are planned. This alternative earned value system is not as robust as the cost-centric system because the task cost performance data are not considered. However, it is predictive of project performance in the same sense that the cost-centric system is predictive: If project activities that cause performance do not change, then the past is likely to repeat in the future, whether for good or for bad.

Defining the Work

In this earned value system, the definition of work packages, the organization of work into the WBS, and the creation of the performance baseline follow the description given for the cost-centric system. The scheduling, consisting of dependencies and resource application, is likewise identical. The difference resides in what is measured for value accumulation purposes.

Measurements of Value

Similar to the planned and earned value measurements of the cost-centric system, the time-centric system applies planned and earned starts and finishes. Table 5-6 presents the definitions in the time-centric earned value system.

Applying the Measurements

Look at the example project given in Figures 5-7 and 5-8 to see the measurements at work. Table 5-7 shows the project results.

TABLE 5-6 Time-Centric Earned Value Measurements

Measure	Definition
Planned start or finish	A task start or finish planned for the reporting period
Earned start or finish	A task start or finish claimed and validated as having started or finished in the report period
Start performance index (StPI)	The ratio of earned starts to planned starts
Finish performance index (FPI)	The ratio of earned finishes to planned finishes

The project manager evaluates time-centric performance in the following way. The first step is to validate the claims for a "start" or "finish." The task leader offers substantive evidence that a start or finish, in accordance with the definitions given in Table 5-6, has been accomplished. The project manager evaluates this evidence and either gives credit or not for the claimed start or finish. Graphs similar to those shown in Figures 5-7 and 5-8 are constructed from the data.

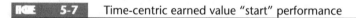

FIGURE 5-7 Time-centric earned value "start" performance

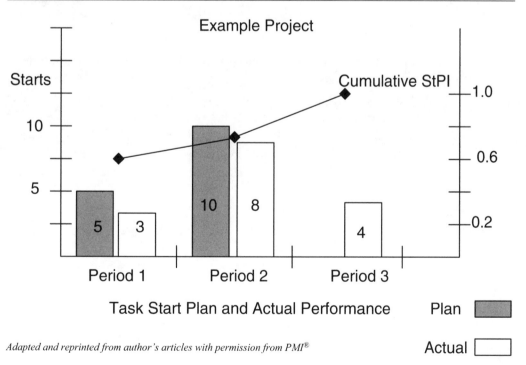

Adapted and reprinted from author's articles with permission from PMI®

FIGURE 5-8 Time-centric earned value "finish" performance

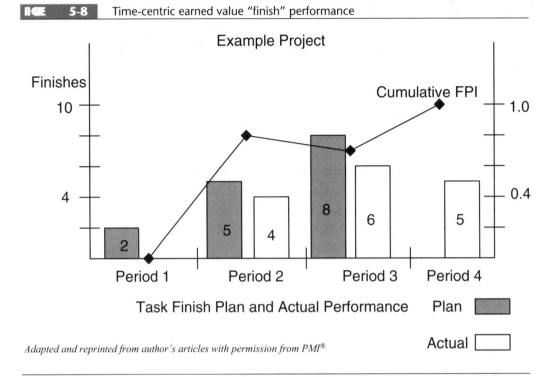

Adapted and reprinted from author's articles with permission from PMI®

As in all earned value concepts, the emphasis is on accomplishment. Indeed, from practical experience in applying this technique, it is all too easy to claim a task start. After all, unless the definition of start is understood to mean a true kickoff of the task, what really is a start? On the other hand, validating claims for finishes is easier. A finish means a deliverable is ready, or the prerequisites for successor tasks have been met.

The second step is to interpret the validated data. From the indices and

TABLE 5-7 Time-Centric Project Results

Planned	Earned	Cumulative Index
Planned starts	Earned starts	StPI
Period 1: 5	3	3/5 = 0.6
Period 2: 10	8	11/15 = 0.73
Period 3: 0	4	15/15 = 1.0
Planned finishes	Earned finishes	FPI
Period 1: 2	0	0
Period 2: 5	4	4/5 = 0.8
Period 3: 8	6	10/15 = 0.67
Period 4: 0	5	15/15 = 1.0

TABLE 5-8 Time-Centric Project Forecast

Planned	Forecast	Cumulative Index
Planned starts	Equivalent starts	StPI
Period 1: 5	3 + 12/.6 = 23	3/5 = 0.6
Period 2: 10	11 + 4/.73 = 16.5	11/15 = 0.73
Period 3: 0	15 + 0/1 = 15	15/15 = 1.0
Planned finishes	Equivalent finishes	FPI
Period 1: 2	0 + 15/0 = Uncertain	0
Period 2: 5	4 + 11/.8 = 17.8	4/5 = 0.8
Period 3: 8	10 + 5/.67 = 17.5	10/15 = 0.67
Period 4: 0	15 + 0/1 = 15	15/15 = 1.0

the accumulation of performance, it is apparent early that the project is going to be late delivering. By graphing the data, or by setting up an array of linear equations for the rate of starts and finishes, the project manager forecasts the schedule outcome. Table 5-8 provides the forecast data for this project. The formula is as follows:

Forecasted schedule = Actual performance + Remaining performance/Index

This formula calculates an "equivalent" performance that is predictive of the effort. For instance, as seen below, in the second period the start performance is equivalent to a project of 16.5 starts, not 15. This suggests a schedule risk of perhaps as much as 10 percent [(16.5 − 15)/15 = 10%]. More pessimistically, the finish performance in the same period suggests a schedule risk of 18 percent [(17.8 − 15)/15 = 18%].

The third step is to develop mitigations for unfavorable forecasts. After all, the motivation for earned value systems, whether this one or any other, is to stimulate action on the part of managers to make changes that will alter the course of performance and bring the project into conformance with the investors/sponsors' value proposition as chartered on the project balance sheet.

- Earned value tools help the project manager measure and assess accumulation of value all the way through the project implementation.
- The main purpose of earned value systems is to give the project manager information sufficiently early that poor performance can be corrected before it unduly impacts value performance.
- Cost-centric earned value systems are robust measures of project performance if the measurement systems are in place to provide the necessary data for analysis.
- Time-centric earned value systems are a substitute for cost-centric systems when the cost collection measures are not available but there is a need to focus on value accumulation.

NOTES

1. Quentin W. Fleming and Joel L. Koppelman, *Earned Value Project Management, Second Edition* (Newtown Square, PA: Project Management Institute, 2000).
2. John C. Goodpasture, "Everything You Wanted to Know about Time-Centric Earned Value," *PM Network*, January 2000 (Sylva, NC: Project Management Institute, 2000), p. 52.
3. Quentin W. Fleming and Joel L. Koppelman, *Earned Value Project Management, Second Edition* (Newtown Square, PA: Project Management Institute, 2000).
4. Ibid.
5. John C. Goodpasture, "Everything You Wanted to Know about Time-Centric Earned Value," *PM Network*, January 2000 (Sylva, NC: Project Management Institute, 2000), p. 52.
6. Ibid.
7. John C. Goodpasture and James R. Sumara, Earned Value--"The Next Generation: A Practical Application for Commercial Projects," *PMI Seminars and Symposium Proceedings* (Upper Darby, PA: Project Management Institute, 1997).

CHAPTER 6

Schedule Risk and Value Attainment

There is no "Undo" button for our oceans of time.

TOM PIKE
Rethink, Retool, Results, 1999

Among the many risks to assess and track, risks to the schedule are paramount. Schedule impacts costs, opportunities, and resources. Schedule delay may compromise quality and impact other project schedules. Controlling cost, exploiting opportunity, delivering quality, and maximizing resources have their roots in managing time. Thus, schedule management couples both project implementation success and subsequent value attainment through operations or product sale. For this reason, this chapter presents schedule risk management and value attainment together.

MANAGING SCHEDULE RISK

Hulett defines the three main purposes of a schedule risk analysis as:
1. Determine the likelihood of overrunning the schedule
2. Estimate the likely exposure or contingency needed to drive the remaining risk of overrun down to a level acceptable to the organization
3. Identify the locus of the key risks in the schedule to guide risk management efforts.[1]

Schedule Fundamentals

In developing a risk-manageable schedule, an understanding of the following scheduling fundamentals is essential:[2,3]

- **Critical path method (CPM) schedules are deterministic.** The duration of the CPM schedule is computed by adding single-point estimates of activity durations along the longest contiguous path through the network. This path is called the critical path. Every logically linked schedule has at least one critical path, but there may be more than one. A critical path has no "float." Any delay of any task on the critical path delays the project end date. The critical path predicts the completion date only if everything goes *according to plan*. This method is limited in accuracy because single-point estimates of durations do not account for performance uncertainty.

- **Activity duration estimates are really probabilistic assessments about what can happen in the future.** That is, when the task leader estimates the task duration, although a single number of hours, days, or weeks, it is in fact an estimate of the statistically "most likely" duration of the task.

- **Near-critical paths are problematic.** Using probabilistic analysis, there is some likelihood that task durations will conspire so that a path that is not the critical path will become critical. Thus, a "near-critical path" is a path that is not deterministically critical, but statistically may become critical, thereby delaying the project.

- **Most likely dates do not add up.** Many believe that using the most likely estimates of duration will yield the most likely completion date. In fact, it will not. A completion date computed this way is not the most likely date. It often is not a date with an acceptable level of risk.

Schedule Primitives

Schedules, as shown in Figure 6-1, consist of the following three basic primitives:[4]

1. **The single task with an activity duration risk.** Each activity appears in the schedule with a duration that represents the most probable number of work periods necessary to accomplish the task.

2. **The path.** A path consists of at least two activities that are linked by a relationship between the task's starts and finishes. The relationship shown in Figure 6-1 is called "finish-to-start." Start-finish relationships are defined in the precedence diagramming method (PDM). More information on PDM can be found in Chapter 6 of *A Guide to the Project Management Body of Knowledge, 2000 Edition.*

3. **The merge point.** This is the point where more than one path joins, typically at a milestone. At such a merge point, the milestone is not complete until all paths joining at the milestone are complete.

FIGURE 6-1   Three primitives make schedules

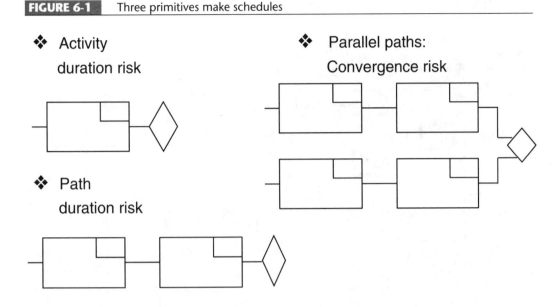

❖ Activity
    duration risk

❖ Parallel paths:
    Convergence risk

❖ Path
    duration risk

Adapted and reprinted from author's articles with permission from PMI®
Adapted and reprinted with permission from David T. Hulett

Schedule Architecture

As the project manager constructs the project schedule from these primitives, schedule architecture emerges. The tasks are formed into major paths; from the dependencies and durations, one or more critical paths are identifiable, and the milestone merge points become visible. As dates are applied to the task's starts and ends, float becomes evident. *Float* is the time difference between the earliest start date of the task and the latest start date of the task that does not impact the completion of the project on time.

Float = Early start date – Latest start sate

where latest start date does not impact project completion. Figure 6-2 illustrates a portion of a typical schedule architecture.

The project manager next evaluates the vulnerability of the schedule architecture to delay, looking for weaknesses that can be made stronger. Each of the five steps involved is discussed separately.

IDE 6-2   The critical path has no float

A(14)   Critical task on the critical path

Task duration in days is shown in parentheses

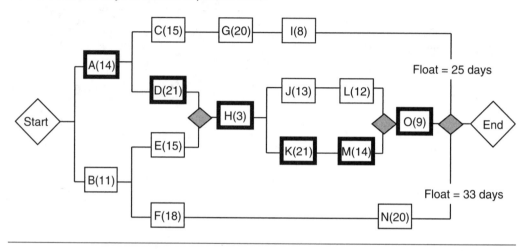

Step 1: Examine Paths of Long Duration

Paths of longer duration are more uncertain than shorter paths because there is more time for unplanned things to happen. From the mathematics of statistics, variance analysis shows that a tandem string of shorter tasks is more certain than one long task of equal overall "most likely duration." Table 6-1 compares the attributes of one long task with a path of two shorter tasks in finish-start sequence. On a CPM schedule, the length of the long task would be shown as 60 days. The length of the two short tasks combined would

TABLE 6-1   Long Task Variance versus Short Task Variance*

Task ID	CPM Duration	Most Likely Duration	Minimum Duration (–10%)	Maximum Duration (+30%)	Average Duration†	Variance (Days²)‡
Long task	60 days	60 days	54.0 days	78.0 days	64.0 days	26.0
Short task 1	26 days	26 days	23.4 days	33.8 days	27.7 days	4.9
Short task 2	34 days	34 days	30.6 days	44.2 days	36.3 days	8.9
Sum of short tasks	60 days	No information available on probability distribution of sum of short tasks			64.0 days	13.8

*Example assumes triangular distribution for all tasks.
†Average = (Minimum + Most likely + Maximum)/3
‡Variance = [(Maximum – Minimum)² + (Most likely – Minimum)(Most likely – Maximum)]/18

also be shown as 60 days. However, under the assumptions in the table, the expected value of the schedule, whether one path or two, is actually 64 days. The uncertainty, as represented by the variance, is significantly less with the two short schedules, however.

The project manager makes an entry on the project balance sheet for the duration of the schedule. Expected value is the best estimator for duration. Thus, 64 days, not 60 days, is carried to the balance sheet for schedule duration. Expected values, means, or averages of tasks in tandem can be added; also, variances of independent tasks in a path can be added.[5] However, when there are joins or merges of tasks that are in parallel, more complex treatment is required.

Unlike means and variances, minimum, maximum, and most likely durations of schedule tasks are actually parametric values of the task's probability distribution function. As function parameters, they cannot be added one task to the next. The adding of nondeterministic "most likely" dates in the CPM schedule is the source of error between 60 days and 64 days. Take note that the average length of the schedule, 64 days, is not improved at all by subdividing tasks. If the statistics of the shorter tasks are the same as those for the longer tasks, this result will hold regardless of how the longer task is divided.

What risk estimates are carried to the project balance sheet? From the example shown in Table 6-1, the variance of the schedule, a measure of uncertainty, is reduced from 26 days squared for the single long task to 13.8 days squared for two short tasks in tandem, a 46.9 percent reduction in variance. If possible, the project manager should replan the schedule with the shorter tasks and put the lesser variance on the balance sheet as the risk. The minimum and maximum durations of the overall two-task schedule cannot be directly calculated; they must be determined by simulation.

Table 6-1 provides an illustration of risk reduction by "risk diversification." The risk of one task is diversified into the risks of two tasks, thereby reducing the overall variance. This same principle can be applied equally well to a list of costs.

Overall, the project manager can reduce cost risk by dividing large cost accounts into smaller accounts that are each managed for least risk. The degree of diversification depends on the size and statistics of each smaller account. For a population of smaller accounts of about the same size and risk, the overall variance is reduced by roughly a factor of 1/N, where N is the number of smaller accounts.[6] The statistical principle at work to make this phenomenon possible is the "method of moments." It says, in effect, that the expected values and variances of independent tasks or costs can be added.[7]

Step 2: Invoke "Rolling Wave Planning"

Often, long durations are an unavoidable consequence of uncertainty in planning. In fact, one planning technique commonly employed is rolling wave planning, in which tasks farther out in time are planned in less detail until a future "wave of planning" occurs. Rolling wave planning defers detail decomposition and planning of long uncertain tasks until a future planning cycle. Figure 6-3 illustrates this point.

Step 3: Examine Merge Points

Merge points are very risky. At each merge point, there are multiple possibilities for something to happen to delay completion of a milestone. In fact, at a merge point there is such a high propensity for delay that it is given a name: "merge bias." Merge bias describes a tendency for the milestone to be delayed, in effect "shifted right." This bias is explained from the mathematics of probabilities as shown in Figure 6-4.

FIGURE 6-3   Rolling wave planning has risks

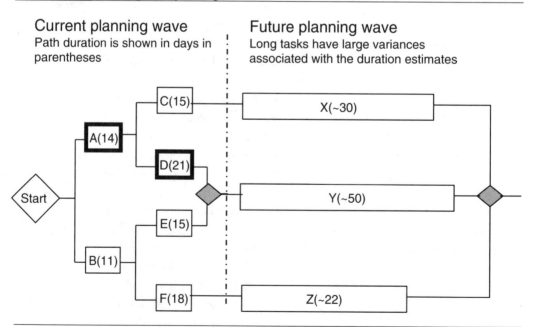

Current planning wave
Path duration is shown in days in parentheses

Future planning wave
Long tasks have large variances associated with the duration estimates

FIGURE 6-4 Merge points are at risk for delay

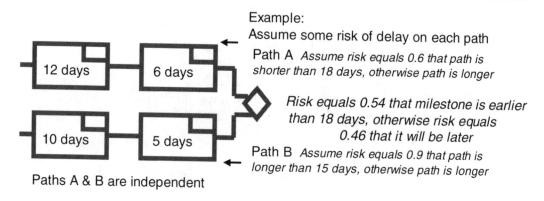

Example:
Assume some risk of delay on each path

Path A *Assume risk equals 0.6 that path is shorter than 18 days, otherwise path is longer*

Risk equals 0.54 that milestone is earlier than 18 days, otherwise risk equals 0.46 that it will be later

Path B *Assume risk equals 0.9 that path is longer than 15 days, otherwise path is longer*

12 days   6 days

10 days   5 days

Paths A & B are independent

Adapted and reprinted from author's articles with permission from PMI ®
Adapted and reprinted with permission from David T. Hulett

Merge points disrupt the method of moments wherein expected values and variances of independent tasks are additive. The mathematics at a joining milestone is more complex. Analysis of a schedule with joins is best left to simulation, as discussed below.

Step 4: Evaluate Near-Critical Paths

Although a CPM analysis will identify one or more critical paths, a CPM analysis does not evaluate the possibility that other paths could become critical. These other paths are labeled near-critical.

How could another path become critical? Tasks on the critical path have no float, or their float is said to be zero. Other paths are characterized by the float they have. Recall that float is the amount of time that a path can slip in time and not impact the completion of the project. But what if uncertainty in task performance leads to more duration or a late start or finish beyond what can be absorbed in the float? Such a task may become critical and impact the finish date of the project. Such a task or path is said to be near-critical. It is a risk that is characterized statistically, as shown in Figure 6-5.

Managing the float in the project schedule is an important task for the project manager. The overall objective is to ensure that the critical path does not become longer, delaying the whole project. To meet this objective, Goldratt[8] introduced the concept of the "critical chain," which is illustrated in Figure 6-6.

FIGURE 6-5	Near critical path is at risk of becoming critical

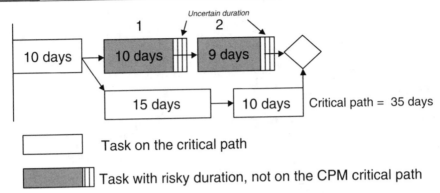

→ Task 1 risk parameters: Most likely CPM duration: **10 days**; estimated expected value of **11 days***

→ Task 2 risk parameters: Most likely CPM duration: **9 days**; estimated expected value of **12 days***

→ Expected value of path "Task 1 + Task 2": 11 days + 12 days = **23 days**

→ Path "Task 1 + Task 2" is nearly on the critical path statistically; it is "near critical"

* The project manager estimates the expected value from the 3-point estimate of minimum, most likely, and maximum duration

FIGURE 6-6	Critical chain buffers uncertainty

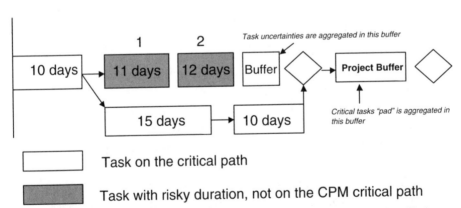

→ Task 1 and Task 2 are scheduled for a duration that has a 50% probability of being longer or shorter*

→ Feeding buffer absorbs risk of duration from Tasks 1 and 2

→ Project buffer absorbs overall project risk

* The expected value duration and 50% cumulative probability duration are not usually the same, except in a perfect normal distribution. For simplicity, the expected values from Figure 6–5 are the 50% cumulative probability durations for this example.

Critical Chain is a concept developed by Eliyahu Goldratt in *Critical Chain* (Great Barrington, MA: North River Press, 1997).

Goldratt proposes the following:
- All task durations be managed to the median of their probability distribution, which is the 50 percent probability of success point.
- "Feeding buffers" of various durations be set to absorb the impact of noncritical task performance on the critical path.
- An overall project buffer be established at the end of the critical path to absorb uncertainties in critical path performance. The time for this buffer comes in part from a contribution from each task made possible by managing each task to its median duration estimate.
- All task activity not on the critical path be made subordinate to the demands of the critical path activities.

Step 5: Perform a Monte Carlo Simulation Analysis

Schedule architecture is best examined for its impact on risk using a tool called Monte Carlo simulation. Monte Carlo simulation "executes" the schedule many independent times, forming a histogram or distribution of schedule outcomes. There is one outcome for each "run" of the schedule that shows the probability of finishing on a specific date. To have a distribution of outcomes, one or more CPM tasks are characterized by a probability distribution that specifies a most optimistic date, a most pessimistic date, and usually the most likely date for that task. Either the beta distribution or the triangular distribution is selected for the task distribution because the asymmetry of these distributions models actual performance quite well. The Monte Carlo simulation follows the process delineated in Table 6-2.

To see how Monte Carlo simulation works, consider the following situation. Barbara is a project manager with a typical software project to manage.

TABLE 6-2 Monte Carlo Simulation

Step	Explanation
Identify tasks that have uncertainty that may impact the critical path.	All tasks have some uncertainty, but the analysis should focus on tasks that present the greatest risk to completing the project on time.
Select a probability distribution and apply it to the task.	The probability distribution is typically beta, triangular, or normal. Depending on which distribution is selected, the parameters of mean, standard deviation, pessimistic, optimistic, or most likely are estimated.
Run the schedule many times.	Each time the schedule is run, the Monte Carlo simulation picks a task duration from the distribution according to the probability that such a duration will occur.
Evaluate the outcome.	The outcome of a simulation is a histogram of possible dates with a probability associated with each date.

It consists of several tasks and a milestone, as shown in Figure 6-7. Uncertain of the overall schedule, wary of the impact of schedule on value attainment, and needing to complete her project balance sheet with the major risks quantified, Barbara runs a Monte Carlo simulation on the project.

Figure 6-7 presents the simulation results with all four tasks in finish-to-start precedence as shown. Barbara assumes each task to be risky, with the risk parameters as shown. A histogram, or probability distribution, of the finish milestone finish date possibilities is shown for 100 iterations of the schedule. The histogram is scaled on the vertical axis such that the sum of all histogram cell values is 1.0. The accumulating sum of the histogram is shown as the "S-curve," which is overlaid on the histogram. The S-curve is functionally the integral of the histogram; it is called the cumulative probability function.

$$S\text{-}curve = \Sigma \; All \; histogram \; cell \; values$$
$$S\text{-}curve = \int histogram, \; as \; cell \; width \; becomes \; infinitesimally \; small$$

FIGURE 6-7   Monte Carlo simulation estimates risk

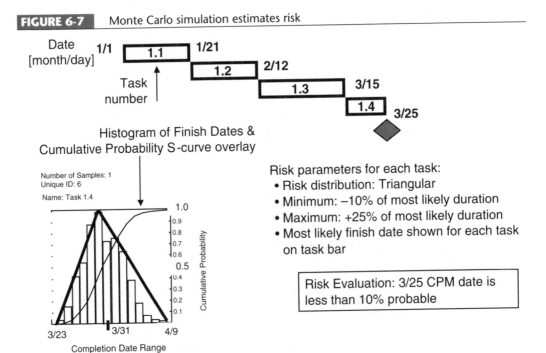

Adapted and reprinted from author's work with permission from PMI®

The S-curve is often interpreted as a "confidence" of meeting a date. To the far right, the curve has a value of 1.0, meaning 100 percent confidence that the milestone date will be the date at this value or an earlier date. The date shown for a confidence of 100 percent is April 9; compare this finding with a 10 percent confidence for March 25.

To compute an expected value for the schedule that Barbara will carry to the project balance sheet, she estimates that a triangular distribution is a good approximation of the distribution of the milestone probability histogram. Using the equation for finding the expected value of a triangular distribution, Barbara calculates that the expected value of the finish date is March 31, or 90 days from project initiation on January 1. Thus, 90 days is the expected value of schedule duration she puts onto the project balance sheet. The uncertainty is from 8 days shorter, March 23, to 9 days later, April 9. These dates bound the project balance sheet schedule risks.

ATTAINING VALUE AND MANAGING BENEFITS

All too often value and benefit attainment must be managed. For this management task, there is a need for a "benefits manager," typically the project investor/sponsor. Recall that project value is derived from goals and that benefits are the means to recover project investment. Value attainment and benefits may not be identical. The benefits manager employs benefits measurement and reporting tools appropriate to measuring investment recovery and invokes key performance indicators (KPIs) to track value attainment.

The Benefits Manager

The benefits manager holds the following responsibilities:
- Define and validate benefits at the time the project is chartered and the project balance sheet is developed.
- Prepare (with the project manager as a partner) the organization to accept and apply the project deliverables in the manner expected to generate benefits and achieve the goals of the project. Table 6-3 summarizes the preparation steps.
- Establish metrics and a process for data gathering, evaluation, and reporting of benefits.
- Establish KPIs for measuring and tracking value attainment.
- Evaluate variances between benefit and value attainment baselines and actual performance.

TABLE 6-3 Tasks to Prepare for Benefit Attainment

Task	Explanation
Communications	Interactively explain to all stakeholders the goals and benefits of the oncoming project deliverables. Objectively answer questions, objections, and concerns. Communicate frequently, early, and objectively. Continue to communicate after roll-out until the deliverable is in the mainstream.
Training	Instruct all stakeholders who have a hands-on relationship to the deliverables about the deployment and application of the deliverables.
Pilot	Selectively apply the deliverables to a group of users to obtain feedback that can be acted on before roll-out to all users.
Rehearsal	Dry run roll-out of deliverables to remove uncertainties of how deliverables will be deployed and applied.
Roll-out	Deploy and apply the deliverables to the users.

- Plan or facilitate plans to correct variances.
- Execute plans.

Sources of Benefits

Project value is a consequence of strategic planning and goal deployment. Once project planning commences, the project manager and the project investor/sponsor work jointly to define benefits.

Project managers and project investors/sponsors often face an important issue about benefits: Some benefits are "hard" while others are "soft." Hard means that there is a directly measurably effect because of a project outcome; soft refers to the fact that the effects in the business cannot be directly measured and associated with the outcomes of the project. Table 6-4 presents typical "rules" for benefit sources.

Benefits Metrics

The mantra of the benefits manager is "that which is not measured is not attained." To obtain benefits performance measurements, the benefits manager must do the following:

- Establish a baseline from which to measure. Analysts validate that the baseline represents a steady-state level of performance.
- Determine the point in time when benefits measurement will commence. Ordinarily, this is coincident with the completion of the project.
- Periodically measure benefits accumulation, forecasting whether or not the benefits objective will be met.

TABLE 6-4 Rules for Benefit Sources

Benefit Source	Source Attribute	Rule
Revenue or sales dollars	–Hard benefit if from new product and services –Soft benefit if from other improvements such as sales administration	Soft benefits are not counted as recovery for hard costs of implementation
Direct expense reduction	Hard benefit	Allowable as recovery of hard costs or soft costs
Retirement of capital plant and equipment		Benefits come from cessation of operating expenses and income from salvage
Changed policy, process, or procedure	Soft benefit unless accompanied by direct expense reduction or plant and equipment retirement	Benefit arises from improved morale, turnover, quality, and throughput; these benefits are avoided costs, which are soft costs
Customer satisfaction	Soft benefit	Usually this benefit is applied after project costs have been recovered by a hard benefit
Innovation and learning		
Personal productivity		

- Analyze the forecast and develop action items to correct any under-performance.

Example of Benefits Management

Susan is the project manager for a capital facilities improvement project for the XYZ Manufacturing Company. This facility is a cost center. The principal source of benefits is headcount reduction due to improved efficiencies that can be applied to the workload. Headcount reduction, a hard benefit, provides cost savings that recover the investment in the new plant and equipment. After recovery of project cost, these hard benefit savings drop to the bottom line. Susan's benefit management plan is presented in Table 6-5.

A benefits report for Susan's project, once deployed and made operational, could look something like the one shown in Table 6-6.

Key Performance Indicators

Key performance indicators (KPIs) measure the effectiveness of the project outcome toward satisfying business goals. In effect, KPIs track the value attainment of the project. For instance, if the business goal of the project is to improve customer satisfaction, and the project introduces new customer service technology, then the cost recovery benefit may come from

TABLE 6-5 Benefit Management Plan for Renovated Capital Facility

Item	Explanation
Benefits manager	The project investor/sponsor accepts the responsibility for benefits management. The investor/sponsor is a senior manager in manufacturing operations to which the facility is assigned.
Rules regarding benefit sources	All sources of benefits must be accountable on a departmental budget plan. Since the facility is a cost center and has no revenue accountability, all benefit sources will be from cost savings.
Benefit metric	The main source of benefits is headcount reduction. Headcount will be measured from human resource personnel assignment records over a calendar year prior to the deployment of the new facility. Average workload will be taken from job tickets whose cost has been accumulated in the general ledger. An average productivity with a standard deviation will be calculated. Average headcount and standard deviation will be calculated and established as a baseline.
Steps to prepare for the new facility	The facility manager is made a part of the planning team. The plan includes, but is not limited to, the following: • Training of operational personnel in the new equipment and process • Steps to complete existing jobs and delay new jobs until the new facility is rolled-out and certified for operations • Dates for all activities that impact operating personnel • Steps to measure productivity that are rehearsed and agreed to by operating managers and supervisors • A process to identify redundant personnel, retrain and redeploy those personnel to other vacancies, or release those employees who cannot be otherwise placed • A communications plan that covers all aspects of the new facility roll-out • A path through the management chain to escalate problems and answer questions

TABLE 6-6 Value Earning Report for Renovated Facility* ($000)

			Report period 1				
Baseline Headcount (FTE)	Baseline Productivity	Current Headcount (FTE)	Benefit Attainment per FTE	Benefit Baseline per FTE	Cumulative Benefit	Forecast for Year
24 average 2.8 SD	22 hours per job 3.6 hours SD	18 average	$2.1 per month in avoided payroll	$2K per month	$12.6 First period report	$2.1/$2 = 1.05 (Ratio > 1 is good)

*Values of independent variables are assumed. FTE, full-time equivalent measured in hours at standard cost; SD, standard deviation.

reduced cost of customer service operations—but the KPI is a measurement of customer satisfaction. To employ KPIs, the benefits manager must do the following:

- Develop KPIs that are measurable and for which there is a reasonable association of cause and effect. Finding this reasonable association is perhaps the most difficult task.
- Place responsibility for KPI achievement with the operational managers who have performance responsibility.
- Identify who is going to make the KPI measurements, how frequently they will be made, and with what tools.
- Determine how the measurements are to be validated, and to whom they are to be distributed.
- Review performance periodically and assign action items to the operational managers involved.

Example of KPI Management

A warehouse management system is planned for the XYZ Company to better control the physical inventory of parts and finished goods. The business case for this project states the goal of raising the quality of inventory management. This means less shrinkage; fewer late, short, and incorrect finished goods shipments; less cost of handling; and greater customer satisfaction with distribution.

The benefits manager parses this business case in the following way:

- Quality and customer satisfaction become KPIs. Cost recovery of the warehouse management system project investment comes from the hard benefits of less shrinkage; reduced transportation costs from fewer late, short, and incorrect finished goods shipments; and less labor cost of handling.
- A quality KPI measure can be developed by employing the "with-without principle" described in previous chapters for cost of quality. A quality index for errors and non–value adding effort also can be developed to demonstrate achievement of the goal.
- A customer satisfaction KPI can be developed by before and after survey methods.

- Risks are uncertain outcomes that are characterized by statistics and managed for minimum impact on the project, particularly the project schedule.
- Schedule risk arises from three architectural features: float of tasks that could impact the critical path, long durations that have substantial statistical variance, and milestone merge points that have a bias toward delay.
- Monte Carlo simulation is the tool of choice for evaluating the impact of uncertainty on schedule outcome.
- Three statistical distributions handle most risk situations in projects: the normal distribution for outcome variations that tend to distribute symmetrically around an average value; the beta distribution for asymmetry that is often typical of real situations; and the triangular distribution, which is a model of the beta distribution, but involves easier computations.
- Benefits and KPIs must be actively managed or they will not be realized.
- Benefits management requires assigning a benefits manager, setting a measurement baseline, establishing metrics, and measuring and evaluating performance against the baseline, correcting with action items wherever necessary.
- The organization requires preparation to receive and apply the project deliverables in a manner that obtains value for the project investor/sponsor.

NOTES

1. David T. Hulett. Seminar materials: *Schedule Risk Assessment and Management* (Santa Monica, CA: D.T. Hulett & Associates, presented June 25, 1996).
2. John C. Goodpasture, "Gap Analysis: How to Get Your Information Technology Project Off on the Right Foot," *Proceedings of the 30th Annual Project Management Institute, 1999 Seminars and Symposiums* (Upper Darby, PA: Project Management Institute, 1999).
3. David T. Hulett. Seminar materials: *Schedule Risk Assessment and Management* (Santa Monica, CA: D.T. Hulett & Associates, presented June 25, 1996).
4. Ibid.
5. Douglas Downing and Jeffery Clark, *Statistics the Easy Way* (Hauppauge, NY: Barrons Educational Series, Inc., 1997).
6. Tzvi Raz and Shlomo Globerson, "Effective Sizing and Content Definition of Workpackages," *Project Management Journal* (Newtown Square, PA), Volume 29, Number 4, December 1998, pp. 17-23.
7. John R. Schuyler, *Decision Analysis in Projects* (Sylva, NC: Project Management Institute, 1996).
8. Eliyahu M. Goldratt, *Critical Chain* (Great Barrington, MA: North River Press, 1997).

Bibliography

A Guide to the Project Management Body of Knowledge, 2000 Edition (Upper Darby, PA: Project Management Institute, 2000).

Anderson, James C., and James A. Narus. *Business Market Management, Understanding, Creating, and Delivering Value* (Upper Saddle River, NJ: Prentice Hall, 1999).

Downing, Douglas, and Jeffery Clark. *Statistics the Easy Way* (Hauppauge, NY: Barrons Educational Series, Inc., 1997).

Finegan, P.T. "Financial Incentives Resolve the Shareholder-Value Puzzle." *Corporate Cashflow*, Oct. 1989, pp. 27-32.

Fleming, Quentin W., and Joel L. Koppelman. *Earned Value Project Management, Second Edition* (Newtown Square, PA: Project Management Institute, 2000).

Goldratt, Eliyahu M. *Critical Chain* (Great Barrington, MA: North River Press, 1997).

Goodpasture, John C. "Everything You Wanted to Know about Time-Centric Earned Value." *PM Network*, January 2000 (Sylva, NC: Project Management Institute, 2000), pp. 51-54.

Goodpasture, John C. "Gap Analysis: How to Get Your Information Technology Project Off on the Right Foot." *Proceedings of the 30th Annual Project Management Institute, 1999 Seminars and Symposium Proceedings* (Upper Darby, PA: Project Management Institute, 1999).

Goodpasture, John C. This example is derived from material developed by the author for the training course "How to Capture Requirements and Develop Project Scope" available from Catalyst Management Consulting, LLC, Findlay, OH (2000).

Goodpasture, John C., and David T. Hulett. "A Balance Sheet for Projects: A Guide to Risk-Based Value Part I and Part II," June 2000, *PM Network*, May and June 2000 (Sylva, NC: Project Management Institute, 2000).

Goodpasture, John C., and Thomas N. Mangan. "A Practical Methodology for Integrating Functional Process Design and Data-driven Packaged Software Development," *PMI '98 Seminars and Symposium Proceedings* (Upper Darby, PA: Project Management Institute, 1998).

Goodpasture, John C., and James R. Sumara. "Earned Value-The Next Generation: A Practical Application for Commercial Projects." *PMI '97 Seminars and Symposium Proceedings* (Upper Darby, PA: Project Management Institute, 1997).

Goodwin, Jonathan. Insight provided to the author that the right and left sides of the project balance sheet are bound by a common understanding of scope (2000).

Hammer, Michael. Seminar materials: *Managing the Process-Centered Enterprise, Principles and Practices* (Boston, MA.: Hammer and Company. Seminar presented December 3-4, 1997).

Higgins, Robert C. *Analysis for Financial Management* (Boston, MA: Irwin/McGraw-Hill, 1998).

Hulett, David T. Seminar materials: "Schedule Risk Assessment and Management" (Santa Monica, CA: D.T. Hulett & Associates. Seminar presented June 25, 1996).

Hulett, David T. The example of risk aversion was provided to the author in a technical note from Dr. Hulett (2000).

Kaplan, Robert S. and David P. Norton. "The Balanced Scorecard—Measures that Drive Performance." *Harvard Business Review*, January-February, 1992, pp. 73-79.

Kulak, Daryl, and Eamonn Guiney. *Uses Cases Requirements in Context* (New York: Addison-Wesley, 2000).

Martin, John D., and J. William Petty. *Value Based Management* (Boston: Harvard Business School Press, 2000).

McQuarrie, Edward F. *Customer Visits* (London: Sage Publications, 1993).

Pike, Tom. *Rethink, Retook, Results* (Needham Heights, MA: Simon and Schuster Custom Publishing, 1999).

Porter, Michael E. *Competitive Advantage: Creating and Sustaining Superior Performance* (New York: Simon and Schuster, Inc., 1998).

Raz, Tzvi, and Shlomo Globerson. "Effective Sizing and Content Definition of Workpackages." *Project Management Journal*, Volume 29, Number 4, December 1998, pp. 17-23.

Schuyler, John R. *Decision Analysis in Projects* (Sylva, NC: Project Management Institute, 1996).

Shiba, S., A. Graham, and D. Walden. *A New American TQM, Four Practical Revolutions in Management* (Portland, OR.: Productivity Press, 1993).

Thiry, Michel. *Value Management Practice* (Sylva, NC: Project Management Institute, 1997).

Tully, Shawn. "The Real Key to Creating Wealth." *Fortune*, September 20, 1993, pp. 38-50.

Index